HERDING TIGERS

ALSO BY TODD HENRY

The Accidental Creative

Die Empty

Louder Than Words

HERDING TIGERS

BE THE LEADER THAT CREATIVE PEOPLE NEED

TODD HENRY

WITHDRAWN

PORTFOLIO / PENGUIN

Portfolio / Penguin
An imprint of Penguin Random House LLC
375 Hudson Street
New York, New York 10014
penguin.com

Most Portfolio books are available at a discount when purchased in quantity for sales promotions or corporate use. Special editions, which include personalized covers, excerpts, and corporate imprints, can be created when purchased in large quantities. For more information, please call (212) 572-2232 or e-mail specialmarkets@penguinrandomhouse.com. Your local bookstore can also assist with discounted bulk purchases using the Penguin Random House corporate Business-to-Business program. For assistance in locating a participating retailer, e-mail B2B@penguinrandomhouse.com.

Library of Congress Cataloging-in-Publication Data

Names: Henry, Todd, author.
Title: Herding tigers : be the leader that creative people need / Todd Henry.
Description: New York : Portfolio, 2018. | Includes index.
Identifiers: LCCN 2017042633| ISBN 9780735211711 (hardcover) |
ISBN 9780735211728 (e-book)
Subjects: LCSH: Leadership. | Management. | Teams in the workplace. |
BISAC: BUSINESS & ECONOMICS / Leadership. |
BUSINESS & ECONOMICS / Management. | SELF-HELP / Creativity.
Classification: LCC HD57.7 .H4466 2018 | DDC 658.4/092—dc23
LC record available at https://lccn.loc.gov/2017042633

While the author has made every effort to provide accurate telephone numbers, Internet addresses, and other contact information at the time of publication, neither the publisher nor the author assumes any responsibility for errors or for changes that occur after publication. Further, the publisher does not have any control over and does not assume any responsibility for author or third-party Web sites or their content.

Printed in the United States of America
1   3   5   7   9   10   8   6   4   2

Book design by Daniel Lagin

For brave leaders everywhere
and the creative people who follow them.

CONTENTS

PART TWO
YOUR MECHANICS

HERDING TIGERS

HOW TO DRAW DARTH VADER

There is always a well-known solution to every human problem—neat, plausible, and wrong.

—H. L. Mencken

Southern heat will make you do crazy things. In this case, the sweltering locale was Disney World, and the act of crazy was ducking into a gift shop to catch a break from the sun. I don't know about you, but I tend to avoid gift shops at all cost. I believe that they are designed solely for the purpose of grabbing me by the ankles and shaking me upside down to claim what's left in my pockets, after I've already spent the equivalent of the price of a nice compact car just to get into the park.

My family strolled the aisles, and I discreetly slid to the side of the store to get out of the way. I found myself standing directly beneath an air-conditioning duct, and as I basked in my personal igloo, my eyes were drawn to a bright red T-shirt a few feet away. At the top of the shirt were the words "How to Draw Darth Vader," and underneath were step-by-step directions for sketching the Sith Lord. (If you'd like to see it, go to toddhenry.com/darth.)

Panel one: "Start with a head and body." (Above was an illustration of a crude body and a simple trapezoid for the head.)

Panel two: "Add a cape." (Again, a crude illustration of Darth Vader's cape.)

Panel three: "Draw the face, gloves, and boots." (A third crude, cartoonish illustration showing the rough outlines of these things.)

Then, the final step.

Panel four: "Add details and some shading. FINISHED!"

Above these words was a *perfectly* photo-realistic drawing of Darth Vader, light-years (ha!) more sophisticated than the previous three panels. I still laugh to this day when I think about it.

I find the T-shirt funny not just because of the surprise ending, but because it is a great analogy for how leadership advice is often dispensed:

"Have a clear vision!"

"Hire talented people!"

"Listen more than you speak!"

And voilà! Brilliant work pops out the other side, no?

Well, no. The *actual* mechanics of leading creative work are way more complex than our neat, plausible clichés can handle. There is very little black and white, or even shades of gray. Challenges to leaders of creative teams appear in shades of brown—a blending of multiple colors to the point that it's difficult to discern what the original colors even were. Creative work must be figured out as you go, and the most sought-after people are those who can shape the chaos into form, meaning, and value. There are no "easy steps" or "magic principles." The "magic" happens between panels three and four, and it's really just the result of a lot of hard work by super-talented team members (who make it look easy).

If you've picked up this book, chances are that you are responsible for leading the kind of work I just described. You have talented, creative people on your team, with all the extreme highs and (occasional) frustrations that accompany them. You spend much of your day figuring out how to harness their collective focus, energy, and creativity to produce value for your organization and your clients. When everything is going well, you love your job, but when the work starts going off the rails, you start wondering whether you should look for a more sanity-friendly line of work. ("I wonder if the post office is hiring? Or the DMV?")

You've probably heard it said that leading creative people is like herding cats. I *strongly* disagree, and I find the analogy demeaning. If you've hired brilliant, driven people, it's more like herding tigers, powerful beings who cannot be corralled but must be carefully, individually, and strategically led. However, many creative leaders I encounter don't have a clear framework for how to do this. They are promoted from within their organizations and suddenly find themselves leading people who were once their peers. Their only example of how to lead is *their* former manager, who was a total jerk (or a pushover, or a brownnoser, or if they were lucky *maybe* was a great leader). So regardless of how talented they might have been as team members, once promoted into a leadership role they find themselves asking: "Now what?"

This book strives to answer that question.

At the risk of telling you something you already know, there is tremendous pressure that comes with leading creative work. You have to juggle multiple stakeholders (your clients, your manager, your team) while somehow discerning the right strategy out of a thousand and one possibilities. You have to manage the egos of the highly talented and opinionated people on your team while simultaneously holding them accountable for their shortcomings. You are asked to stretch limited resources into something ("Superb!" "Amazing!" "Stupendous!") that the world's never seen, all while keeping your team sane and prepared for the next project kickoff, which is in, oh, a few days. And, as an afterthought, you also have to somehow manage your own career aspirations. In short, you are asked to do the near impossible.

And you probably love it. It's in your blood. Even in your most frustrated moments, you wouldn't have it any other way. You get to work with gifted people doing unique work for (generally) appreciative people. However, that doesn't lessen the stress that results from a few unique challenges that leaders of creative work experience.

Opacity. At some point, you've probably heard the phrase "Let's let the 'creatives' handle that." It's as if there were some mythical box where complexity goes in one end and amazingness comes out the other. You're handed problems and told to "do your magic." Often, this is because the creative process is opaque to your stakeholders and clients—they don't see the many decisions that you had to make and the ideas you chose *not* to act upon. They often just see the result. To some extent, this can be an advantage because you don't have to justify every choice you make. On the other hand, it can also work against you when you are expected to work miracles with too few resources and too little time. Worse, if you go above and beyond and exceed everyone's expectations once, those expectations rise next time ("You did it last time—why can't you do it again?"). As the leader, it's your job to shine a bit of light on the process and help your stakeholders understand your team's abilities, capacity, and constraints.

Insecurity. It's not always the case, but often with creative people comes the ever-so-unpleasant parade of big egos and big insecurities. There is a tremendous amount of personal risk and vulnerability involved in doing creative work. Because the work is highly visible, when you ask the people on your team to try new things and step outside their comfort zone, it means that they instantly become a target for critique. If someone on your team is leading with her ego, she might become defensive about her ideas, dominate every meeting, and remain closed off to information that runs counter to her "gut." If someone is leading with his insecurities, he will play it safe and refuse to stand up for his ideas, even when he knows he's right. Either way, people aren't bringing their best ideas and work to the table.

As the leader, it's your job to manage the delicate balance of ego and insecurity on your team and to challenge people to lay down their guard in the pursuit of the team's mission. You have to be part drill sergeant, part fan club president, and part therapist. Mainly, you must carry the fire for your team and speak life and courage into its work so that team members feel permission to take risks and grow.

Subjectivity. Oh, and by the way, your final product will likely be judged by someone who gives you either a thumbs-up or thumbs-down, often based on little more than personal opinion or that of a committee of stakeholders. Even when based on research and sound reasoning, creative work is frequently qualitative in nature, so it can feel like you are shooting at moving targets while simultaneously switching weapons. On top of this, you have to manage the shifting expectations of your manager, client, and team while steering them toward a resolution that will satisfy everyone. (No pressure.)

Because of these unique challenges, creative leadership can feel lonely, and it can seem that no one else understands the pressures you face. You take criticism for unpopular decisions even though you know they are in the best interest of your team. You have to make snap, high-consequence judgments in the face of uncertainty because, well, *someone* has to do it. Unbeknownst to everyone around you, you regularly sacrifice your own ego in order to allow your team to stand in the spotlight, because it's the right thing to do.

But please know that your sense of being alone is a lie. There are countless others who are out there braving the storm and striving to do right by their team and their clients. Also know that it is possible to have a thriving team that communicates clearly, fights in a respectful and productive way, pulls together at critical moments, and strives to do work that pleases your client *and* that you are creatively proud of as well. To get there, your team needs you to lead.

You see, although everyone wants to *be* the leader, far fewer are willing to actually lead. Leading is about more than just hitting your objectives; it's about helping your team discover, develop, and unleash its unique form of brilliance. That's why, although all good leaders are effective, not all effective people make good leaders.

A good leader of creative people accomplishes the objectives while developing the team's ability to shoulder new and more challenging work. Both are essential. If you accomplish your objectives, but the team requires your direct input on every decision, then you've failed to hit the mark; you are a bottleneck, and your team is probably cursing your overcontrolling nature behind your back. If your team consistently hits its objectives but isn't growing creatively, you're just teaching your people *how* to do things without teaching them *why* the tactics work. They will eventually grow bored and leave.

I spent the formative years of my career on both sides of the equation: as a creative pro and as a leader of creative teams. It's tough to do work that you're proud of while also juggling organizational issues. Frankly, I was overwhelmed (read: terrified) when I first stepped into a leadership role, and I wish I'd had the benefit of a book like this to show me I wasn't alone. (That's why I'm writing it!) I've also had a unique perch over the past decade as I've worked with creative teams and leaders across dozens of industries, listening to the stories of their struggles, their successes, their failures, and their aspirations. During that time, I've interviewed super-talented leaders from diverse industries about how they do what they do. This book aims to share what works and addresses many of the complaints I've heard from creative pros about where their leadership is failing them. In fact, many of the stories in this book are from people who have cornered me to share their experiences.

Now, it's important to note that no book can offer complete, tailor-made advice for you or your organization. I'm not trying to. All advice is local. Instead, I'm aiming to provide you with a handful of frameworks through which to see your own choices as a leader, as well as some very specific tactics, conversations, and rituals to help you gain better focus, protect your margin, and earn trust from your team. Adapt them as needed. Some chapters may not resonate right now, whereas others will convince you that I've placed a hidden camera on your office wall. (Look over your left shoulder—hi!) That's how it should be. Your situation is unique. My hope is that you'll revisit this book as new issues arise and when you need to remind yourself that you're not alone. Perhaps you'll pass it on to peers and even your team in order to discuss how you can create a healthier, more focused culture.

In order to lead others effectively, you

Although everyone wants to *be* the leader, far fewer are willing to actually lead.

must first lead yourself. Despite your great intentions, all of your qualities—both good and bad—are only amplified through your leadership. As goes the leader, so goes the team.

This means that if you want to reach your full ability as a leader, you must get your internal and external worlds aligned. To deal with the chaos of creative leadership, you need firm footing, which is precisely what the remainder of this book is designed to help you obtain.

REFINING YOUR LEADERSHIP MIND-SET

When you transition from a frontline role to a leadership role, you must make a major shift in how you think about your work. You are no longer responsible solely for your own projects, your own career, and your ideal workload. Instead, you must focus primarily on how to equip and resource others. You will be tempted to control the work of your team by stepping in and doing it yourself or by telling people what to do instead of letting them solve their own problems. Engaging in these bad habits—often out of insecurity—only shrinks the capacity of the team. This approach doesn't scale beyond you.

In the first part of this book, you will learn about the basic mind-set shifts that effective creative leaders make and how to reinforce them with regular checkpoints. Some of these principles are counterintuitive and certainly countercultural, which is why many leaders fail to embrace them. That's also why the first several chapters (2 through 5) will require a bit of deep thought and personal introspection. Shifting your mind-set is difficult, especially if you already have a bit of leadership experience under your belt. I'm warning you in advance that you'll be tempted to skip over concepts and not engage with the questions. *Don't.* Those who are willing to spend some time with these chapters will go to another level in their leadership and will win the trust and respect of their teams.

DEVELOPING YOUR LEADERSHIP MECHANICS

What you know matters little if you don't put it into practice. Great leaders have great rituals. In the second half of the book, I'll describe practical methods for honing your team's focus, managing team members' time, and maintaining trust, as well as weekly, monthly, and quarterly practices that reinforce your ability to lead. You'll see how intentional conversations can defuse tension before it explodes. You'll also learn how to manage your team's energy so that team members aren't going through the constant cycles of crash, burnout, and refresh that plague so many creative teams. You'll see how the best leaders inspire their teams with new ideas and help team members spend their time on effective activities, not just efficient ones, so that they're making investments in the future.

As a side note, I know that you're probably already buried in work. The last thing I want to do is pressure you with new exercises, conversations, and rituals. Through-out this book there are dozens of such things that you can apply to help you in your role, but please don't allow my suggestions to overwhelm you. Take what resonates and is useful, and implement those first. Then implement a few more. This book is intended to bring you freedom, not to create a whole new layer of work.

Great leaders have great rituals.

However, the strange paradox of creative work is that freedom often comes through structure. You need boundaries to define how you spend your focus, time, and energy. That's why it's important to have rituals that anchor your life and your leadership.

THE RITUALS

When researching to write a book about creative leadership, you quickly discover that everyone has an opinion. However, I tried to heed advice from my grandfather: "If you want to know someone, don't ask what they think, watch what they do." Therefore, I tried to observe the specific tactics and rituals that great leaders use to help them gain clarity and unleash their teams' creative brilliance. In general, the end of each chapter breaks down these rituals and practices into three buckets: weekly, monthly, and quarterly. Taking just a little bit of time on a regular basis to check your mind-set and mechanics will ensure that you never veer too far off course.

Weekly rituals are designed to help you review the patterns of the past several days and plan for the following week. They will mostly guide you with tactical decisions about which conversations you need to have with team members, which tasks you should be focusing on, and which priorities should be occupying the majority of your mind space.

Monthly rituals are designed to help you consider larger patterns, including team dynamics and resource allocation, overall team focus and energy management, and team health and inspiration. The rituals that you engage in monthly are perhaps the most important to the operation of your team.

Quarterly rituals are primarily about you, your leadership, your own development, your goals, and where you are leading your team and yourself over the coming months. They are designed to help you take a longer look at your ambitions, areas of potential misalignment in your own life and on your team, and how you might need to reallocate your focus, assets, time, and energy over the coming quarter to better position you for success.

Readers of my previous book *The Accidental Creative* will notice that these rituals correspond with the checkpoints (weekly, monthly, quarterly) that I recommended in that book. Over the past several years, I've received many comments from leaders saying that they had adapted the checkpoints in *The Accidental Creative* to their personal leadership needs. Some of the practices in this book are actually derived from what these leaders reported worked well for them. Others are practices that I learned from the leaders I interviewed in the course of my research. All of them are tactics from the front line, designed to help you close the gap between panels three and four.

HOW TO READ THIS BOOK

First, a warning: I'm going to expect a lot from you. The stakes are simply too high for you and your team for me to speak vaguely, and chances are you're not looking for more inspirational slogans to hang on your office wall. You need practical, tactical ideas that will help you gain clarity and will take your leadership to the next level. That's what this book is designed to give you. Because of that, it might feel a little overwhelming at times. There are many questions to answer and exercises to engage in, and you simply won't have time to do all of them at once. Do the ones that fit your current situation and skip the ones that don't. However, do *something*. It's not what you know that's going to change the game for you and your team; it's what you do about it that matters.

That said, some chapters may resonate deeply with where you

are right now, and some chapters simply may not click as much. That's perfectly fine. I encourage you to move through the book at your own pace and to engage in whatever way best meets you where you are at the moment. If you need to read half a chapter at a time, or just a section, that's great—do it. This isn't a race, so take it at your own pace.

One more thing: talk to your team about the concepts in the following chapters. If you'd like to read and discuss the book as a team, you can download a free workbook at:

toddhenry.com/herdingtigers

There, you can also sign up for the Leader List, which is a short, weekly e-mail newsletter designed to help you apply the book's principles throughout the year.

IF YOU DON'T LEAD, WE LOSE

The decision to lead, by *someone, somewhere,* is the point of origin for every great thing that has ever existed. You only discover what you're truly capable of as your influence scales.

I hope that this book helps you to be brave, to pour yourself into your team, and to realize your full measure of influence in your life, your organization, and the world. Most of all, I hope that you choose to embrace the leadership mantle and to dedicate your life to unleashing the brilliance of the creative people on your team, because in doing so you will create a body of work that extends far beyond your own reach.

CHAPTER 1

WHAT CREATIVE PEOPLE NEED

A company in which anyone is afraid to speak up, to differ, to be daring and original, is closing the coffin door on itself.

—Leo Burnett

PRINCIPLE: There are two things creative people need more than anything else: stability and challenge.

First, let's discharge the myths about creative people that saturate the workplace. You may not think you believe any of them, as you were probably the target of these same myths at some point in your career, but it's easy to fall into the trap of generalizing the people on your team when you're under pressure to deliver results. You've probably heard something like: "They're just so difficult," or "You have to treat them *soooo* carefully," or "Don't bruise their precious egos."

Yes, there are certainly creative pros who regularly exhibit behaviors that feed these myths. In fact, you might even work next to someone who exhibits all of the behaviors I describe below. The problem is, we often use the isolated behavior of a few dysfunctional people to make broad assumptions about entire groups. Further, the problem with many workplace stereotypes is that they often point to symptoms rather than the core issues.

Perhaps some creative people *appear* to be difficult because the expectations for a project keep changing midstream, after they've done a tremendous amount of conceptual work that will have to be rehashed just to get back to the starting line.

Is it possible that what comes across as ego is merely a response to their craft's—which they've spent years mastering and cultivating—being challenged at a moment's notice by someone who has given their hard work a total of ten seconds of distracted consideration before scrapping it?

Much of the dysfunction and tension that exists in the work-place is the result of highly creative people's needs not being met. If you step back and examine the patterns, you'll find that a lot of bad behavior occurs when there is poor or inattentive leadership.

FIVE MYTHS ABOUT CREATIVE PEOPLE

There are a handful of commonly held misunderstandings about creative people that I regularly encounter when talking with leaders. Like any stereotype, there are some elements of truth in all of them, but they oversimplify reality and create a lot of roadblocks to healthy collaboration. In addition, when you hold any of these myths to be true, even subconsciously, it can affect your ability to give your team what it truly needs from you.

Myth 1: Creative people just want total freedom. I hear this all the time from leaders who come from less traditionally "creative" roles. There is a standing belief that creative people want to remove all boundaries so that they can have a wide-open field to play in. This perception is often the result of creative people on their team having pushed back against overly constrictive boundaries or challenged a direction with which they disagree, but it's not indicative of what most creative people truly want or need from their leadership.

The truth is that creative people want boundaries. They *crave* boundaries. A wide-open playing field is not helpful to the creative process. Although it sounds strange to many people, the most common complaint that I hear from creative people is that they lack a predictable environment in which to do their work. (More on that below.) They know that they need clearly defined boundaries and resources so that they can focus on doing what they do best.

However, when forced to choose between being overly restricted and completely free, creative people will choose freedom, which is not always in their best interest. Thus, striking a healthy balance is your role as the leader, and it's essential to good collaboration.

Myth 2: Creative people care only about how "cool" the idea is. Another persistent myth is that creative people aren't concerned with the result, and they just want to work on something that feels cool and edgy and lets them exercise their creative muscles. This is also largely untrue. Most of the highly creative people I encounter are professionals and are very concerned with results. They understand that results equate to revenue, which equates to more work (and an on-time mortgage payment).

However, they also get frustrated when an obsession with practicality means prematurely sacrificing creative possibility. Settling quickly on the easiest and most apparent answer and then moving straight to execution might seem like an efficient use of resources, but it often means failing to bring the best thought and effort to the project, which is demoralizing to the team. Over time, this approach is a recipe for burnout and turnover, both of which cost the organization dearly.

Myth 3: Creative people lack analytical ability or business acumen. I've heard the equivalent of "Just focus on making things look good, and let me worry about the strategy" tossed out in a meeting. Not in those words, of course, but the sentiment is still there. The truth is that most creatives have a well-honed analytical process, which is essential to their creative process. It is often a circuitous one, analyzing many sides of the problem at once, rather than the linear, straight-line analysis that many strategists use. Consequently, it often yields insights that others have overlooked.

> **The truth is that creative people want boundaries. They *crave* boundaries. A wide-open playing field is not helpful to the creative process.**

The kind of systems thinking that creative people provide is of tremendous value to the organization and should be welcomed at the table during strategic discussions. As we'll see in a later chapter, inviting input into the process is also a way to reinforce trust on your team.

Myth 4: Creative people are either egomaniacs or completely insecure. It's important to distinguish between actions and traits. Yes, many creative people respond to a change in an important project or to a difficult conversation by posturing or leading with their egos. Some completely retreat into themselves and need constant reassurance that they're on the right track. However, don't think that this is how they would prefer things to be. Many creative people have developed learned responses to unhealthy organizational dynamics, and they are simply acting out of self-protection.

Again, this isn't always the case. I've run into some remarkable egomaniacs out there, and there are some people who lack simple self-confidence. However, more often than not these exhibitions are an attempt to communicate that there is something they aren't getting from you or the organization.

Myth 5: Creative people tend to be flighty or flaky. One of the common misconceptions about highly creative people is that they are quick to jump ship when a more interesting idea comes along. They will work hard until they are no longer interested, and then they'll lose interest and phone it in so that they can work on the idea they really like.

The truth is that most highly creative people are extremely committed to their craft or area of specialty, but they can certainly be distractible if not led well. There is a method to their madness, though, and because they tend to be more aware of stimuli in the environment and tend to be able to make loose connections between them more easily, they can quickly get off track. This isn't a bug; it's a feature. This awareness and ability to see patterns can be of tremendous benefit if it can be channeled into the work that the organization values. However, you need to do your job as a leader and regularly communicate your values, the problem you're trying to solve, and the existing constraints for the project so that the team understands its parameters well.

I realize that I have been painting with a broad brush. Are there creative people who want total freedom? Of course. Are some flaky and unable to focus? Sure. Are there creative people with overinflated egos? You bet. However, holding these broad stereotypes about creatives does more damage than good, and you can't let them persist inside your organization. You need to fight for and defend your team. Every creative pro is unique and will have to be strategically and intentionally led, but there are a few things that most of them need in order to thrive.

WHAT CREATIVE PEOPLE NEED: STABILITY AND CHALLENGE

As a leader, there are two key things that creative people need from you more than anything else: stability and challenge. Stability means that the environment around them is as predictable as it can reasonably be so they can focus their creative instincts on solving the actual problems the work presents instead of wasting them trying to resolve the uncertainty of the work environment. Challenge means that they are given the chance to engage in work that stimulates them, allows them to grow, and instills a sense of personal accomplishment.

The Components of Stability

To be clear, stability doesn't mean that there will never be last-minute changes or unexpected curveballs. Of course that will happen. You cannot predict client demands or organizational shifts every time. However, your team needs to see that you are doing your best to create an environment in which those distracting and demoralizing shifts are kept to a minimum so that they can pour themselves fully into their work. There are two key components of stability that you should focus on, and that I'll be addressing in various ways throughout the rest of the book: clarity and protection.

Clarity. Your team needs you to be clear about your expectations, even when you are uncertain that they are the right ones, so that they don't have to worry about rework or wasted time. Many leaders waffle or get very unclear when they are uncertain because they don't want to be wrong or they are trying to protect themselves. This is the kiss of death in creative work, because ideas that lack precision lack punch. They will wither and die. If you want your team to do great work, you need to take the first risk by giving it clear direction.

Take Stephen, for example. He was a designer for a small creative team. Because of the time-consuming nature of his work, even slight changes to the direction of a project could mean hours of rework, even though it didn't seem like a big deal to the organization's leaders. However, the problem wasn't the changes; it was the cavalier way in which they were made. It was typically late in the project before leaders would make a subjective decision about what they liked and what they didn't, which meant that Stephen would have to come in early or stay over the weekend to keep the project on track for delivery. Stephen came to resent these changes; he wasn't angry because the decisions were made, but because they were entirely avoidable if there had been more diligence in setting clear expectations early in the process. Instead, there was always a "wait and see" approach, and Stephen was inevitably the one who paid the price. Over time, he lost his passion for his work and would simply wait for his manager to tell him what to do rather than putting much effort into the early stages of the project. This meant, of course, that the team wasn't getting the best out of him, and his own personal satisfaction with his work plummeted. It was lose-lose.

Even if Stephen's manager had given him clear direction from the start, had worked to get buy-in from the organization's leaders at key moments in the project timeline, and had fought to keep everyone focused and invested throughout the process, it's still possible the direction might have needed to change at some point. However, Stephen wouldn't have felt devalued and taken for granted and would likely still be a thriving member of the team. Clarity about expectations and stability would have made a huge difference in his experience

If you want your team to do great work, you need to take the first risk by giving it clear direction.

and the quality of his work. Unfortunately for the organization, Stephen has since taken his talents to a company that better appreciates the unique challenges of creative work.

Clarity also means providing your team a predictable space in which to do its work. Creativity requires healthy, well-defined boundaries. Unbounded freedom is not helpful, especially when doing work that requires risk. Are there clear terms of engagement, systems, processes, and principles for collaboration, or are they perpetually shifting with the political winds of the organization? Do you back up your words with actions, or is your team constantly wondering when the other shoe will drop? Is it clear what your words actually mean, or is there dissonance between perception and reality?

Finally, your team needs to know what you value, what that means with regard to your expectations, and how that behavior will be rewarded. There's nothing more demoralizing than spending weeks working on what you believe to be a critical project only to realize that it didn't really matter as much as you had originally thought. Similarly, it's maddening to work hard and play by the perceived rules of the team only to find out that the game was rigged from the start, and you're never going to get the promotion that was dangled in front of you.

You want your team focusing on the uncertainty *out there*, not the uncertainty within your own organization. Clarity allows team members to have the mental bandwidth to do their job with excellence.

Protection. Stability is not just about clarity. I can yell to you:

"Hey! I have a really clear view of a crouching lion that's about to attack!" while standing at a safe distance, but it doesn't really help you. You also need my protection, which I am in a unique position to provide because my point of view gives me advance warning that you don't have. Your people need to know that you have their back and that you will stand up for them when the time comes. This means that you are willing to fend off needless organizational demands and ensure that they have the time and bandwidth to focus on doing their most important work. It also means standing in the gap for their ideas and defending your team instead of throwing people under the bus when things go awry.

A young account manager told me that one of her managers always spoke bravely in meetings about how he stands up for the team and would empathize with what it had to go through because someone higher up in the organization had changed his mind. All of those brave words counted for nothing when one day she overheard him casually blaming the team for a failure that was really *his* fault, and she realized that his protective stance was just posturing. In truth, he was selling out the team for the sake of his own career.

If you want the team to take risks and do great work, people need to know that you have their back. You have to stand up for them, and you can never throw them under the bus. The quickest path to irrelevance as a leader is to sell out your team *one time*. If you do, you will never regain its trust.

The other element of protection is using your leadership perch to protect the resources and space your team needs to do great work. Although you can't ward off every outside influence and demand, you can make every attempt to intercept those demands before they rob your team of its precious focus, time, and energy. People need to see you consistently going to bat for them, not just protecting your own self-interest.

Again, you cannot provide a perfectly stable environment for your team. The workplace is rife with uncertainty, and there are tectonic shifts (and just plain difficult clients) you cannot avoid. However, adopt the mind-set of protector in the areas where you hold sway and don't allow the preventable stuff to steal from your team.

When your team lacks stability, whether that means a lack of clear expectations or a sense of vulnerability because it isn't being protected, people are likely to take a "wait and see" approach, similar to the one Stephen took in the story above. This likely means that the team's most fertile creative time, which is at the beginning of the project when possibility is still abundant, will be wasted. Instead, people will simply home in on whatever is practical once a direction is finally set.

They're not going to take a creative risk until you do first. And you can't expect them to. After all, if you're not willing to stick your neck out, why should they? And that leads us to the next important thing that your creative team needs from you: challenge.

The Components of Challenge

In general, creative people love to be challenged. They thrive when doing work that causes them to use new muscles and experiment. They want to feel like they are pushing to the edge of their abilities while still maintaining control. However, challenge isn't just about throwing your team into the deep end of the pool and walking away. There's much more to it.

Permission. Your team needs your blessing. Team members

want to know that you not only want them to take risks, but that you expect it from them. They need to hear from you that you want them to stretch their skills and develop new ones. If they don't sense permission from you, they might do these things anyway, but it will always be while looking over their shoulders. They will rarely go all in, which is likely to result in subpar, rehashed work.

Once, when I was leading a creative team and sensed that it wasn't feeling as much permission from me as I'd like, I created a bumper sticker that read "Safety Is Not an Option," and I plastered it all over the office. (In retrospect, a *bumper* sticker dismissing the importance of safety was probably not the best form for the message. But I digress.) The sticker was intended to communicate that safe, predictable work was unwelcome and that anything that didn't make people feel a little bit nervous was probably too "down the middle." Of course, I didn't mean that they should throw caution to the wind and take stupid risks, but my words gave implicit permission to try new things and live with the gut-churning feeling of probing new territory. Everywhere they turned, they saw that message reinforced.

Without your express consent, your team will always worry about whether they are venturing too far out of bounds. Demand calculated risk, and remind them often. However, you also need to set clear expectations for your team so that it understands the kinds of risks you want. Again, to experience full freedom, your team needs clear boundaries. This allows people to put their full effort into the work without worrying about whether they are unknowingly crossing a line.

Perhaps the most important signal of permission is an environment in which it's not only acceptable but expected to challenge the process, ask questions, and walk headfirst into conflict instead of shying away from it. When you reinforce a culture in which ugly truth is discussed rather than buried, then is worked through as a team, it creates a bond of trust that is difficult to break. Your team members need to feel explicit permission to say what's on their mind, in a respectful way, so that everyone can get on with the work instead of dancing around the real issues.

Faith. Finally, creative people need to believe that you have faith in them. They want to know that you believe they are capable of accomplishing what you've charged them with, because there will be times when they may not believe it themselves. They will rely on you for encouragement. A key way that you signal your faith is by allowing them to *own* their work rather than micromanaging them. Challenge them; then allow them to do what they do best, with regular feedback loops and an open door in the event they have questions or issues.

Not only that, but you have to back up your words with actions. Faith that is merely spoken isn't real. You can say wonderful things about people's abilities, but if you still tend to look over their shoulders every minute of the workday, then they won't believe you. As anxiety inducing as it may be from time to time, you have to cement your faith in your team by establishing expectations, clearing the path, and then getting out of its way.

People who lack challenge will grow bored and begin to drift to greener pastures, fearing that their best work is dying inside them. However, if you keep their fire stoked, pushing them to take risks and grow creatively, then you will earn fierce loyalty through good times and bad.

We could call this combination of stability and challenge a kind of "bounded autonomy." There is freedom of action and decision and a degree of challenge presented by the work itself, but that freedom is bounded by clear expectations, principles that guide the creative and decision-making processes, and established and fair timelines for completion of the work.

The Challenge/Stability Matrix

Your creative team needs both challenge and stability in order to thrive. Sure, it can get by for a season without one or the other, but if left without one (or both) for too long, the team will eventually begin to wither. This is because creative work requires a high degree of emotional risk, meaning that the people doing the work are putting some amount of their own intuition, expression, and worldview into it.

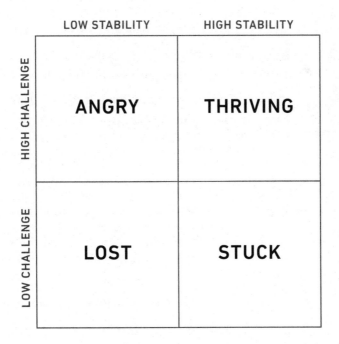

HIGH CHALLENGE + HIGH STABILITY = **THRIVING**

When your team has a healthy mix of stability (clear expectations, established systems, protection from peripheral demands, etc.) and challenge (permission to take risks, work that pushes it, freedom to ask questions), it comes alive. You've created fertile soil in which it can grow deep roots and thrive. Creative teams operating in an environment of high stability and high challenge are poised to produce their best work.

HIGH CHALLENGE + LOW STABILITY = **ANGRY**

When your team has a high degree of challenge but low stability, your team will grow tired of the unclear expectations, last-minute work thrust upon it, and low level of protection from organizational politics. Over time, team members will become jaded and angry that their talents are being used for the benefit of someone else in the organization while they are considered dispensable. Over time, you will train them to simply wait for you to tell them what to do instead of taking initiative and owning the work.

As anxiety inducing as it may be from time to time, you have to cement your faith in your team by establishing expectations, clearing the path, and then getting out of its way.

HIGH STABILITY + LOW CHALLENGE = **STUCK**

It's great to have a measure of predictability about your work, but when it comes at the expense of challenge, creative people get bored quickly. You might think that you're doing the right thing by not pushing your team too hard, and there are certainly seasons in which you should create margin for your team (more on that in a later chapter), but that season can't last too long; otherwise, your people will go looking for greener pastures. They will feel stuck.

LOW STABILITY + LOW CHALLENGE = LOST

I've never encountered a team that stayed in this quadrant for any length of time, except those in companies that are on the brink of going out of business. However, suffice it to say that when creative pros experience no stability in their organization, and there is no challenge to the work, they feel lost and overwhelmed.

As you consider the state of the people on your team, which quadrant do you think best describes them at the moment? Are you encountering a lot of anger and frustration from your team? It could mean that there is a lack of stability and that people don't sense the clarity or protection they need from you. Is your team bored or stuck? It could mean that people don't feel appropriately challenged. (I hope that no one reading this falls into the "lost" quadrant, but if so, it might be time to job hunt.)

Understand that creating an environment in which your creative team can thrive isn't just about increasing job satisfaction and personal accomplishment. There is a tremendous return on investment in maintaining a healthy, functioning, and productive team rather than having to constantly hire and train new employees. On top of that, when the team gets the stability and challenge it needs, the creative people on your team will produce work that is of greater value to your organization and clients and thus will help you achieve your career goals as well. It is a win-win all around, but it begins with you dedicating yourself to being the kind of leader the creative people on your team need. To do that, you must focus on your mindset and your mechanics.

PART ONE

YOUR MIND-SET

CHAPTER 2

STOP DOING THE WORK

The Shift from Maker to Manager

The price of greatness is responsibility.

—Winston Churchill

PRINCIPLE: To create stability, shift your mind-set from doing the work to leading the work.

As the leader, it's no longer your job to *do* the work of the team. Yes, you probably earned your reputation (and your promotions) because you are exceptional in your field, and you may be more technically skilled at the work than many people on your team. True, there are times when you *could* step in and do a task much better than someone else. Yes, if you don't intervene, it's possible that the work may suffer, at least in the short term. However, despite the short-term benefit you might get from swooping in and saving the day, you are probably causing more long-term damage than good.

This is the critical concept upon which everything else in this book rests. If you persist in doing the tactical work of your team, you are failing it as a leader. When *you do* the work, the capacity of your

31

team never scales beyond you—you are training your team to defer to you instead of letting it grow into its potential. Once you assume a leadership role, your job performance is no longer measured by your personal accomplishments. Instead, your job is to unleash the creative potential in others.

Therefore, the first mind-set shift that you have to make as a leader of creative people is from maker to manager. Your job is not to *do* the work; it's to *lead* the work. You probably already know this, even if you're not practicing it, but there are subtle ways in which you can get pulled back into the work and, thus, fail your team.

Take Jason, for example. He is a manager of a midsized team of designers and writers. I was chatting with him one day about how things were going, and he told me things were a little rough at the moment. I asked him to elaborate, and he told me that some team members had approached him and told him that they wanted a little more space to do their work. He went on to say that he felt like the team members were overreacting and that there was way too much ego involved. He sensed that certain team members were worried he might stake a claim on their work and that they wouldn't get the credit they deserved on a high-profile project. He candidly revealed to me that he felt like he was really the only one who could get it right—that if he didn't step in, he'd have to go back and redo their work anyway.

"Why do you feel like you need to micromanage them?" I asked. "Don't you trust them to do their jobs?"

Amazingly, he confessed to me that he didn't. Plus, he knew that his reputation was on the line, and he wasn't going to let his team ruin his chance for promotion. It turns out that Jason had been burned by a few bad hires early in his career and had internalized the message that if he wanted to do something right, he needed to do it himself. However, because he was insecure about how the work would reflect on his reputation as the leader, he would always step in and dictate what needed to be done to "get it right." At some point on every project, his team would inevitably hit a ceiling, because team members never attempted something they didn't believe would square with how Jason would do it. They would simply wait for him to tell them what to do.

Jason's insecurity as a leader was placing an artificial cap on the growth of his team. In essence, their world had shrunk to the size of Jason's perspective, and the result was that his team was frustrated, unmotivated, and underperforming.

When *you do* the work, the capacity of your team never scales beyond you.

Jason's story is not uncommon. He knew deep down that what he was doing was squelching his team's growth, but he fell prey to the pressure to get results now at the expense of future productivity. Sure, as a leader it's more efficient for me to just tell you what to do, but that's not going to help you become great in your role, and it's not going to help me sleep at night when you're handling a major project.

The story above is but one example of the tension that you will face daily as you transition from a maker to a manager mind-set. There are no easy answers, so you must learn to navigate these tensions.

GOOD ENOUGH NOW (MAKER) VERSUS GREAT LATER (MANAGER)

Do you jump in and dictate what your team should do (like Jason above), or do you allow your team to learn from its mistakes and grow? For many leaders, this is a difficult challenge because it might mean allowing a temporary dip in quality in order to allow your team to develop its skills. Even though the latter is the smart, long-term strategy, it can often create a lot of tension in the short term when you're facing pressure to deliver results *now*.

For instance, one leader told me that she was given verbal permission from her own manager to allow her team to take some risks and even to make some mistakes, but whenever the pressure was *really* on, that permission was quickly quashed, and the expectation became "just make it great now!" That caused her to feel torn between helping the team develop its skills and appeasing her manager. She felt pressured to get directly involved and do the technical tasks necessary to produce a great product, whatever it took. This not only kept the team from owning its own work, it created constantly shifting expectations. Trust was broken, and trust is the primary currency of creative teams.

You need to loosen your grip on the work for your team to grow creatively, or it will forever be limited to the scope of your direct involvement.

PRESSURE DOWN (MAKER) VERSUS PRESSURE UP (MANAGER)

You will receive a lot of pressure (down) from your manager, and your manager's manager, to stay within resource constraints and to hit certain marks with the project. They are not concerned about how much the team loves the idea it is working on. Instead, they are primarily concerned with keeping the client happy and winning new business. However, you will also experience a lot of pressure (up) from your team members who want to try new ideas, experiment, take risks, and push boundaries. That's what creative people do best.

You are caught squarely in the middle, with a need to lead in both directions. (We'll talk more about that in chapter 6.)

This often means that you have to balance the practical need to say "it's good enough" with your team's desire to push the limits of what's possible and try risky things. Not every project can be a big risk, but you do need to protect your team's ability to challenge itself by dreaming big. Most creative people need permission to play a little bit with a project; otherwise, they will get bored.

CAREER MANAGEMENT (MAKER) VERSUS TEAM ASPIRATIONS (MANAGER)

You will also experience the pressure of managing your own career while simultaneously subverting your own ambitions for the sake of your team. Great leaders freely credit success to their teams, which sometimes means taking a lower profile role on the winners' podium so that others can mature in their own careers. However, you also have to be mindful of not allowing others to take advantage of your humility or overtly swipe credit for things they didn't do.

Although many organizations *say* "Just take care of the team, and we'll take care of you," the reality is often much different. In some organizations, an invisible leader is a forgotten leader, and it's possible that you could become seen as expendable if the value you bring to the table isn't perceptible to your leadership. This is especially true in creative work, in which each individual's contribution is often diffused because it's difficult to measure. Ensure that you are still managing your career effectively while fulfilling your role as a leader to unleash the best in the people you lead. (This is a tricky balancing act that we'll address more in chapter 12.) The clearer you get about your *true* role as a creative leader, the easier these tensions are to navigate. Clarity comes when you focus on what your team *really* needs from you. You need to step back from doing the work and instead focus on providing three things.

YOUR ROLE: FOCUS, FUNCTION, AND FIRE

So, then, if you're not supposed to *do* the work, then what exactly is it you do every day?

Your job is to provide your team with three things: focus, function, and fire. If at any given time your creative team is not operating like a well-oiled machine, it's likely because it is lacking one of them. Simply considering each on a regular basis can yield valuable insights into areas where your team might be struggling.

Focus means ensuring that your team's attention is allocated to the right problems at the right time. In creative work, there are a million directions your team could go with any project. Team members need effective "rails" to help them channel their efforts so that they don't get distracted by very cool, but unhelpful, ideas. Your team has finite attention to spend on behalf of outcomes that matter. Therefore, how you spend your attention is critically important to your success, which means that you have to constantly define (and redefine) its field of vision.

Focus is primarily about how you answer three questions:

What are we doing? This is not a trick question, and it's not as obvious as it seems, because you can answer it on multiple levels. What we're doing with this specific task or project might be answered differently than what we're doing overall in terms of client strategy. Your job is to ensure that everyone on the team has a crystal clear understanding of what a successful outcome looks like on every level. Further, as we will see later when we discuss focus, creative work primarily consists of problems to be solved, not projects to be completed. As the leader, it's your job to define those problems clearly and ensure clear accountability for solving them.

What are we NOT doing? This is an equally important question. Strategic pruning of priorities is necessary to your team's ability to focus. They have to understand what is *not* a priority during a particular season. If not explicitly spelled out, your team's attention might drift to whatever shiny object comes along. You should dedicate time on a weekly basis to pruning your priorities, and you should ensure that your team knows clearly what you expect it *not* to be doing.

When are we doing it? Expectations around timing affect the choices that a team member makes throughout the day. Ensure that everyone has a clear sense of urgency about the right things and understands how to prioritize the work. These time frames can shift frequently, so don't assume that everyone on your team read the fourth paragraph of the tenth e-mail you copied them on this week, which stated the new deadline for phase two of the new project. You need to have a ritual of scanning the work for shifting priorities and communicating those frequently to the team.

Function is about ensuring that your team has the resources and processes in place that it needs to do its work. Your job is to assess the team's operations and ensure that it has what it needs to accomplish the areas of focus spelled out above.

Function is about how you answer the following questions:

How will we do it? Ensure that there is a clearly defined and articulated path to accomplishing your objectives. That doesn't mean that there won't be unexpected problems or hiccups along the way, but your job is to ensure that the system itself isn't the bottleneck.

Clear obstacles out of the way and stay a few steps ahead in order to spot potential problems before they become big issues. Creative people need the stability of a clearly defined playing field in order to feel safe to do their best work.

What do we need in order to do it? Is there anything that the team lacks? This could be materials, information, or, especially, buy-in from someone on high. Although your team may have to do without important resources during the process, it should never be due to a lack of planning. You have to go to bat for your team and ensure that it has what it needs and that people feel free to ask for resources. Make sure that you keep your eye on your team's needs and keep the lines of communication open so that people can tell you when they've hit a resource-related roadblock.

Fire is about keeping the team motivated to do the work. There's nothing more demotivating than busywork. When you are pouring yourself into something but have no clue why you're doing it, it's a recipe for burnout. As the keeper of the flame, you have to diligently tie *what* the team is doing to *why* it is doing it.

Fire is about answering these questions:

Why are we doing it? Yes, the client asked for it, or your manager's manager has declared it essential, but why are we *really* doing it? What difference will it make to our team, to the company, or to the world? Highly creative people need to understand the bigger pattern, or they might mentally check out. Do your best to tie expectations to something deeper than "because I say so" or "because it'll make the company money."

What will it mean? Great leaders also understand that people are motivated by different things. It may be a shocker to some, but not everyone wants to change the world. (Gasp!) Some people simply want to do work they are good at, pay their mortgages, and find joy in collaborating with others. Help them understand what success on a given project will mean to them on a personal level. This means learning to speak their motivational language not as a means of manipulation, but as a means of helping them kindle their own fire.

When you don't provide one of these three elements (focus, function, fire), you may not notice anything for a while, just like failing to change the oil in your car probably won't matter for a few months. And then, one day, you'll find yourself stranded by the side of the road in the rain and with no cell coverage. This could manifest as a big team meltdown right before a client presentation or a public argument over something that seems meaningless to everyone else. The reality is that small amounts of misplaced focus, toleration of poorly functioning systems, or a lack of "fuel for the fire" create latent pressure in the system that eventually explodes into something much more serious.

As the keeper of the flame, and you have to diligently tie *what* the team is doing to *why* it is doing it.

It's a good idea to review the questions above on a regular basis to ensure that you're not failing to provide focus, function, and fire for your team. If any of the above seven questions lack a definitive answer for you, then you can bet your team is probably confused as well. However, when these questions are answered clearly for your team, you greatly improve your odds of success.

Unfortunately, asking those questions can be more difficult than answering them. You need to have some mechanism for tracking how your team is doing and ensure that you're giving it what it needs (focus, function, fire) at just the right moments. To do it, you need two things: a personal scoreboard and a personal dashboard.

YOUR METRICS: THE SCOREBOARD AND THE DASHBOARD

Imagine that you've decided to drive from Boston to New York to connect with some old friends. It's very important that you're not late, because you have hard-to-come-by reservations at an exclusive Manhattan restaurant that evening, and there is no way it will hold your table. You make all of the preparations for the trip, pack your things, and plan your route. You learn that it typically takes a little over three and a half hours to make the trip by car, and because you're planning to stop once along the way to rest, you decide to round up your expected driving time to four hours.

Of course, the projected trip time is based solely on the assumption that you'll be driving at the speed limit, and, unfortunately, the speedometer in your car is broken. You don't have time to have it fixed before the trip, so you're going to have to drive without it.

Here's my question: How will you know how fast to drive to ensure that you'll be on time for your dinner reservations with your friends? With a broken speedometer, it will be difficult to know whether you're truly on pace or not.

If you're a conservative driver, you might simply stick to the right lane—with all of the slow people—just to ensure that you don't accidentally go too far over the speed limit and get a ticket. Although this strategy will keep you out of trouble with the law, the downside is that you have no way of ensuring that your pace will actually get you there on time.

If you're a more assertive driver (like me), you might stick with the flow of traffic in the fast lane, and you're more likely to get to NYC in plenty of time. However, there is always the chance that an ambitious patrol officer might flag you, adding unexpected minutes to your commute and potentially resulting in a late arrival.

Despite your best efforts, neither of these tactics would assure you of accomplishing your true goal: arriving at the restaurant in time for your reservation. Without a speedometer, it's nearly impossible to know whether you are on pace. You'll have to watch the clock as you drive, check the occasional mileage signs on the highway, and do some quick math to see how you're doing. In the end, you'll only know whether you're successful when you check the time upon arrival, which doesn't really do you much good if your friends have just ordered dessert.

It's not much of a stretch to say that your drive from Boston to New York is analogous to completing a long-arc creative project. You typically have a defined time within which to complete the work and a clear objective you need to accomplish. However, many people go about their work with the equivalent of a broken speedometer. The objective is defined (the "scoreboard," or getting to dinner on time), but they have no way to measure their progress along the way because they lack a clear "dashboard" (a speedometer) to tell them how they're progressing.

Effective creative leaders maintain both a scoreboard and a dashboard for their work, even if they do it informally. These tools help them track important aspects of their team's progress, health, and culture. They also help measure how successfully they, as leaders, are providing focus, function, and fire. These tools are not (necessarily) shared with the team, but rather are something leaders use to help them determine the state of the team at any given time.

SCOREBOARD: WHAT YOU *MEASURE*

Your scoreboard is a concrete indicator of whether your team has accomplished its goals. It helps you (and thus the team) get really clear on what you should be aiming for—for example, "Revenues hit $10 million," or "We won a new client's business." Another way to say it is that your scoreboard consists of trailing measures. You only know after the fact whether you've accomplished what you set out to do.

I recommend that you ask three questions, at regular intervals (such as after each project), to help you track how your team is scoring:

Did we accomplish our objective(s)? In other words, have you solved the problem that you committed to solve at the outset? If so, how do you know? If not, where did you fall short and why?

Did we maintain our values in the process? Succeeding in the short run is of little use if you sell out everything you care about in the process. Did you manage to maintain your principles (see chapter 3) and operate in a way that you can be proud of? If not, did you learn something that you can apply next time?

Are we poised to do it again? It's rare that a team is pulled together to accomplish only one goal. Typically, you'll be tasked with leading your team through a series of projects in order to move the organization forward. So at the end of every project it helps to consider whether you are able to reengage, or whether the process left you reeling. If an army is decimated in battle, it's hard to consider any ground taken as a true victory.

When discussing a completed project (or a season) with your team, you can use these three questions to determine whether you put "points on the board." If any of these cannot be answered in the affirmative, no points are warranted, and there should be a discussion about where things went off the rails so that you can correct for next time. Was it a lack of focus, function, or fire?

DASHBOARD: WHAT YOU *MONITOR*

The scoreboard is the most concrete way to determine success or failure, but it cannot be the only way you measure how your team is doing. If you want your team to be prolific, brilliant, *and* healthy, you must also establish key measures on your dashboard to help you gauge progress along the way, making micro-adjustments as necessary.

The dashboard helps you monitor how your team is engaging with the work. It consists of measures like how aligned your team seems to be, whether the right conversations are happening at the right times, and overall energy level and enthusiasm. These are leading measures, or key indicators that you are headed in the right direction.

Leading measures are often difficult to correlate to the goal. For example, a car's dashboard might include things like oil pressure, engine temperature, RPM, how much gas is in the tank, and speed. Individually, none of these things tells you whether the car is going to get you to your destination, but collectively they tell you how the car is functioning in the moment and whether it needs maintenance. If you ignore the dashboard warning lights for too long, your car will eventually break down and need more costly repairs. The same holds true for your team. You might accomplish difficult objective after difficult objective,

If your only measure of success is whether you crossed the finish line on time and under budget, or whether the client is pleased, you might very well hit your objectives while destroying your team in the process.

all while ignoring the warnings on the dashboard, but eventually you will find that your team is burned out, unmotivated, and largely incapable of engaging when it matters most. Without a dashboard, it's easy for a leader to grow numb to the needs of the team.

Though you will probably engage in conversations with your team about items on your dashboard, it is primarily a personal tool that you use to keep your finger on the pulse of the team. What you measure may change from season to season, as the needs of your team or the demands on its time and energy change. For example:

Pace. Is the team moving too fast to adequately do the work? Do you sense that you are moving too slow and are starting to fall behind on your critical projects? Have a conversation with team members about how they feel about the current pace of work, but also take note of minor deadlines that are missed or the state of breathlessness with which everyone rushes into a meeting.

Health and energy. Have you been on a long run of difficult work? Are team members rested or fried? Have you just taken a big hill, or are you at base camp? All of these things affect what your team needs from you in any given season and the level of engagement you should expect. Watch for frayed nerves or agitation, bags under eyes, and irritation at the most minor request. All of these should be warning signs on your dashboard.

Engagement/enthusiasm for current project load. How connected to and excited about the work is your team at the moment? This is a difficult thing to measure and can only be determined through intentional conversation, both on the team and at individual levels. Watch for redundant or uninspired ideas, disengagement during meetings, or an obsession with distractions and side work. It could be that your team is getting bored and needs an injection of inspiration from you (fire).

Psychological safety. Does your team feel comfortable sharing controversial ideas or hard truths? Or are people stifled by an environment in which speaking out is discouraged? Kirk Perry, president of brand solutions at Google, measures his team's psychological safety via regular organizational reviews. During one review, he learned to his surprise that the team's score was lower than expected, which led him to make changes in his approach to group discussions and his management style. These adjustments were only possible because Perry had been monitoring his dashboard and could make them before there was more critical damage.

Efficiency of communication. If there is a lot of "wait and see" in terms of key decisions on projects or communication from people with whom you're collaborating, then it can stall momentum and ultimately affect your ability to get things done. Do you sense that your team is running efficiently on all cylinders, or is there something preventing you from working together smoothly? Watch for delayed approvals, postponed meetings, and unanswered e-mails. You may need to step in and improve the function of your team's process.

These are only a few examples of dashboard elements that you might want to consider. Your dashboard is likely to be determined largely by the nature of the work you are leading and the maturity of your team. Also, over time your dashboard monitoring might become second nature, though I encourage you to maintain a list of dashboard items as a reminder and to regularly review it. Throughout the book, you'll find many questions, recommended conversations, and checkpoints that you can use as "watchpoints" for your dashboard.

A FINAL CAUTION: STILL GET YOUR HANDS DIRTY

Although it's not your job to do the work of the team, it's also not a good idea to remove yourself from the work *completely*.

Exercise: As you consider your job of providing focus, function, and fire, what do you think should be on your scoreboard and dashboard? Take a few minutes to list some of the things you should be measuring (scoreboard) and monitoring (dashboard) during the current quarter.

You need to stay connected enough to the work to maintain your credibility. If you are going to issue directives about the work from time to time, which you are, then the team needs to see that you are still personally invested in what's going on and that your perspective is still relevant. One senior executive at a large design firm told me that having a pet project or two in which he does some of the technical work is critical to his staying relevant to his team and empathizing with its plight. Otherwise, he would be just another executive issuing orders from on high, with no clue as to what it actually takes to get things done. He told me, "Getting out of the work takes you to irrelevance really quick. Suddenly, all of your stories are old stories. As soon as you lose relevance, you are a caricature. You are talking around the work, but not really talking *about* the work."

Make sure that you have at least a project or two in which you are still doing a bit of the technical work so that you stay rooted and relevant. That doesn't mean doing other people's work for them, though.

As a leader, you need to turn your creative energy from doing the work to thinking creatively about the team dynamics. The transition from maker to manager is one of the most challenging leaps for new leaders to make, because it feels like you are ceding control over your own destiny.

You need to stay connected enough to the work to maintain your credibility.

In truth, that's *exactly* what you're doing.

Put your faith in the capabilities of the people on your team, and dedicate your days to helping them unleash their best work. That's the only way they will grow into their potential and the only way you will grow into the full measure of your influence. Ralph Nader once said, "The function of leadership is to produce more leaders, not more followers."

And then, once you remove yourself from the work, you need to make another transition: from owning just *your* stuff to owning *everyone's* stuff.

CHECKPOINT

Your team needs you to lead, which means providing them with focus, function, and fire. The more clear you get about your true role, and the more your team sees you delivering what it needs from you as a leader, the less margin you will have to worry about your insecurities and shortcomings.

Actions

—Identify one task or piece of work that you've been doing yourself because you're afraid to let go of it. Find someone on the team to take responsibility for it, and get it off your plate.

—Create your scoreboard and your dashboard. Take thirty minutes at some point to identify the following: what are our key measures of success right now (scoreboard), and what team dynamics should I be monitoring (dashboard)?

Conversations

At an opportune time, ask your team any of the following questions that seem appropriate to your situation:

—*What else do you need from me right now?* This is a difficult question to ask, because it is a vulnerable one. However, simply offering your team a chance to air their desires will give you a better sense of where their collective minds are. And you'll see whether there's an outage in focus (what are we doing?), function (how are we doing it?), or fire (why are we doing it?)

—*Is there any place where you're confused about our objectives or my expectations?* Offer your team a chance to show you where things aren't adding up. Everything might be crystal clear to you but thoroughly confusing to your team.

—*Is there any place where I am suffocating you and not allowing you to do your best work?* Ask your team members to be honest about places where they need you to back off so that they can feel freedom to grow and assume more ownership.

Rituals

These rituals are also collected at the end of the book under weekly, monthly, and quarterly categories.

Weekly: Do a mental sweep of the past week for times when you shifted into maker mode versus manager mode and consider how it affected the team dynamic.

Monthly: Review your scoreboard and dashboard and revise them as needed.

Quarterly: Choose one or two projects that will give you permission to stay directly involved so that you don't become too disconnected from the work.

CHAPTER 3

THEY BROKE IT, YOU BOUGHT IT

The Shift from "My Stuff" to "Our Stuff"

No snowflake in an avalanche ever feels responsible.

—Stanislaw Jerzy Lec

PRINCIPLE: To create freedom, shift your mind-set from control to influence and from personal to total accountability.

As a creative leader, you're responsible for more things than any individual can reasonably be expected to juggle. When you're a team member, you only have to worry about what's on your own project list. If something seems broken, whether it's a relationship, a system, or a client interaction, it's not your problem. As long as you get your own work done, you can point a finger at who's to blame for the rest of it.

There are now no fingers to point, except the one aimed at your own chest. You're responsible not just for the things you see, you're responsible even for the things you don't. The culture of the team—the parts you created and the parts you inherited—are all yours as well.

This means that you can no longer just think about how your actions affect the immediate sphere around you. There is now an entire interdependent ecosystem that shifts when you sneeze, and unless you're a two-year-old toddler, you can't be everywhere at once. (OK, in truth a toddler can't either; it only *seems* like it.) However, as we saw in the last chapter, that doesn't stop many leaders from trying to meddle in every decision their team makes.

Effective leaders understand that once they step into their role, they own everything that happens on the team, even if it was out of their direct control.

However, when you try to control bright, talented, creative people, they will eventually seek better horizons, because they'll get tired of running into your overly constrictive ceiling. Instead, effective leaders establish clear principles for how they want the work accomplished, then allow their team members the space they need to work their magic. Again, bounded autonomy.

The mind-set shift from "my stuff" to "our stuff" has two key parts: from control to influence, and from personal to total accountability.

FOR CREATIVE WORK, INFLUENCE SCALES (BUT CONTROL DOESN'T)

Brian Koppelman is the co–executive producer and showrunner for the hit Showtime series *Billions*. Most often, Koppelman told me, the showrunner is the creator of the show and is in charge of every aspect of the production. He is responsible for making sure that everyone is on the same page and that the finished product is consistent with the original vision. He also hires the writing staff, oversees

When you try to control bright, talented, creative people, they will eventually seek better horizons, because they'll get tired of running into your overly constrictive ceiling.

the writing of the episodes, hires the directors of each episode, and is in charge of the casting process. As if that weren't enough, the showrunner is also responsible for planning the shooting days and for the postproduction, musical scoring, and any and all other aspects of the finished product. In other words, if it happens, it crosses the showrunner's metaphorical desk at some point.

Though he and his business partner, David Levien, strive to be deeply involved in all aspects of the show, from writing to postproduction, having "the buck stops here" responsibility for such a massive undertaking means that Koppelman can't possibly be everywhere at once. He says that the only way to lead such a diverse team of creative people is by ensuring that the driving vision is clear, then letting people do what they were hired to do.

Because their vision is clear and well communicated, and their team understands how and why they make creative decisions, Koppelman and Levien are able to lead their collective of super-talented people via influence rather than needing to micromanage every aspect of the production. The result is that everyone on the team is able to freely add a unique perspective to the project without waiting for explicit permission for everything. Koppelman said, "You want to make sure that a director owns the vision for an episode, that it's her show. Yes, you want it to fit within the overall vision, but you have to make certain that she feels like she owns the idea and execution. Otherwise, she will be calling you every few minutes."

Many leaders prefer to control their team because it eliminates uncomfortable conversations and the potential for short-term failure. It's easier to dictate the terms and get exactly what you want, here and now. However, you're also unknowingly robbing future value in order to claim a little present value. Your team will not grow, and you won't attract great people.

So how do you tell whether you are currently leading by control versus leading by influence? Here are a few ways.

Influence Is Leading by Vision; Control Is Leading by Sight

When the goal is to grow your influence over time, you're willing to accept some short-term failure in order to achieve long-term success, because you're working toward the longer-term vision of growing your team's capacity. You set broad, vision-based guide rails and allow your team to work within them, understanding that temporary shortcomings are to be expected as people push themselves and try new things. When you lead by control, any shortcoming is intolerable, so you clamp down and correct any mistake before it can reflect on you.

Your creative guide rails should attempt to inform decisions, not to control and tightly restrict them. Your objective is to teach *how* to think about the work, not *what* to think about it.

Influence Is Situation Agnostic; Control Is Situation Specific

Leading with influence means that team members are taught principles that they can apply broadly to any number of similar circumstances. Control is always situation specific, so when team members get out of

Freedom (within boundaries) is an essential ingredient to creative growth.

familiar territory, they don't know what to do and have to wait for instructions.

Influencers teach principles; control freaks deal in absolutes.

Influence Is About Care; Control Is About Self-interest

When you genuinely care about people, you do your best to set them up for success even when they are no longer under your leadership. You want them to learn how to take on increasing amounts of responsibility and to grow their own influence, maybe even surpassing yours. Control, on the other hand, is all about ensuring that they don't embarrass you or stain your record in the here and now. You just want to ensure that they don't mess everything up for you, regardless of whether they advance in their own careers.

Influence Is About Spreading Praise; Control Is About Claiming Credit

When you lead by influence, the team gets acclaim for any successes. Control is ultimately about putting yourself at the center of everything, which makes it appear that you are the only person capable of making the project successful. Brian Koppelman told me that it's common practice in Hollywood for a showrunner to rewrite even a tiny portion of a script and then claim equal credit. However, even when doing a complete overhaul of another writer's first draft, Koppelman takes a different approach. "One of the strategies that David and I have employed is that if you wrote the draft for something, no matter how much we rewrite it, your name stays on the draft and your name is on the screen, and no one will ever know how much of the original draft we rewrote." This spreading of praise leads to fierce loyalty from the creative people on his team.

Controlling behavior never leads to results beyond your own direct input. However, when you lead by influence, you multiply your efforts and reproduce your values in the lives of others. The key to moving from control to influence is to establish a leadership philosophy, or a set of guiding principles, which clearly communicates what you value, how you make decisions, and what's most important for the team and the work.

YOUR LEADERSHIP PHILOSOPHY

Do you have a leadership philosophy? Is it clear to your team how you make decisions and why you make the ones you do? Influential leaders establish clear principles by which they and the team will make decisions. Your set of principles is the clear point of view that you share with your team members to help them understand what you expect, how you make creative decisions, and how you want them to interact with the work.

In Ray Dalio's book *Principles*, principles are defined as "concepts that can be applied over and over again in similar circumstances, as distinct from narrow answers to specific questions." Your principles allow your team to work without your needing to be involved in every single conversation or decision. They are the single best method for scaling your influence.

In creative work, a good set of core principles is necessary because it offers your team stable boundaries within which to explore and play. To feel free to take creative risks, your team needs to know that there is some predictability about the process itself. When everything is up in the air, including the framework by which decisions are made, it's difficult to make intuitive leaps, because you never know if there will be ground under you when you land.

As you begin to think about your own set of principles, here are a few, well, principles to guide you.

Principles are specific enough to provide guidance but general enough to allow for creative application. The goal with principles is to convey the guiding philosophy for making decisions but to allow enough freedom for people to apply them as they see fit. For example, "Do great work" is too broad. However, "Great work means a quality end product + a healthy process + taking strategic risks" is more useful because it gives the team something to measure its work against.

Principles are reflective of culture but are personality agnostic. Your leadership philosophy should reflect the culture that you want your team to have, but it shouldn't be centered on you. Ideally, the principles will live on long after you've moved on to another role (or organization). Don't create a cult of personality around yourself, or your influence will begin to die once you move on.

> To feel free to take creative risks, your team needs to know that there is some predictability about the process itself.

That said, make sure that you infuse your values into the principles as well. If there are things that you believe to your core, then bring them out into the light. It's the only path to integrity as a leader. Show your point of view. If you like something, say so. If you strongly dislike it, don't hide it. When you keep people guessing about your opinions, it decreases team stability.

Principles may be in tension with one another but still belong together. On the surface, it may seem that certain principles in your leadership philosophy contradict each other. For example, "Speak the truth, always" and "Only reveal necessary information at the right time" could appear to be in conflict. What if I know something that could affect the project, but the information is not yet ready for public consumption? In this case, not sharing the information means I'm violating a principle, and so does sharing it. Remember that principles are not rules. Principles don't dictate action. Instead, they provide a framework to help people deal with the baked-in complexity of creative work. This leads to the final thought.

Principles provide guidance but do not replace thoughtful action. Finally, principles are not "Set it and forget it." Every situation you'll face as a creative pro is unique. As such, the principles serve to guide you and your team, but they are not an instruction manual. They exist to convey the values of the team and to create accountability for the kinds of choices that are made, but they cannot dictate those choices. That's why it's a good idea to review your principles on a regular basis and do a refresher with the team on why they are important.

HOW TO ESTABLISH YOUR PRINCIPLES

Your set of principles *is* your point of view as a leader. It's the means by which you exert your influence over the decisions your team makes.

You don't have to write a volume of leadership beliefs. It's better if your set of principles is simple, direct, and easily memorable. For example, one former vice president at a research consultancy told me that one of her earliest leaders gave her two core principles by which to work: "Make mistakes of commission, not omission," and "Believe that I have your back when you make a mistake." She said that this simple leadership philosophy gave her permission to take strategic risks without the fear of reprisal, which often led to innovation and, thus, company growth. She knew that it was far worse to fail a client because of a failure to act than it was to fail that same client by taking a calculated risk. In addition, she knew that in the event of a failure, the leader was going to go to bat for her and wouldn't "throw her under the bus" in order to protect his own reputation. This infused her work with boldness and allowed the team to produce far greater value for the client, because it wasn't afraid of failing.

Your leadership philosophy can be as simple as a few directives, like the example above, or it can be more extensive. Here are a few questions that can help you establish your own principles. Plan a half hour at some point this week to jot down five answers to each.

What kinds of behavior do you celebrate every single time, regardless of the outcome? Is there something you will always celebrate even if the project "failed" in the traditional sense? "Take calculated risks" is one example. Even if the result isn't considered a success according to the original objectives, the risk itself is worth celebrating as long as you learn from it.

What are the rules of engagement? Are there specific principles for collaboration that you want people to honor every time they engage in a project? Your team members need a set of principles by which to relate to one another and work together on projects. "We always defend one another in public, regardless of whether we agree in private" is an example. You might not like another person's idea, but you will defend that person in front of the client in order to maintain team unity and create a safe environment to think potentially dangerous thoughts. "We speak truth directly to one another" serves as a principle to avoid private commiserations and potentially harmful gossip.

How do you set priorities? Is there a certain kind of work that generally should take precedence over another? For example, do you drop everything to deal with a customer issue, or do you instead prioritize the project work? How much of your time should be spent in meetings, and who gets to call one? Everyone on your team should be able to answer the question "What is the most important thing we do, regardless of how urgent something else feels?"

How do you differentiate between good work and bad work? What are the qualities that you look for in good work? How do you know when something isn't quite hitting the mark? Infuse these principles into the culture so that team members are able to discern for themselves when a project is completed, or when it needs to be sent back into the process for further refinement.

Drafting your leadership principles can take time, and you should only share them with your team when you believe that they are clear. There's nothing worse (or more confusing) than working out your principles in public. Set aside some time in the next week to begin the process.

FROM PERSONAL TO TOTAL ACCOUNTABILITY

It's no longer sufficient to be solely focused on the work. You must now consider how your decisions affect the Work (with a capital *W*), meaning the work of the entire team. This means considering how every demand you make will affect its ability to perform. It's easy to call a meeting every time you have a question or to stop by and interrupt someone to offer an opinion. However, any of those little interruptions can feel like a major train wreck to the team's workflow. Every casual,

You must now consider how your decisions affect the Work.

impromptu meeting you call has an equal and opposite reaction to a project that's nearing deadline, not to mention the stress level of the person responsible for it.

But the mind-set shift is about more than meetings. As a leader, you have to shift your total mind-set from the work to the Work. You need to think carefully and with empathy before acting.

Pause before making a decision or making a request of your team, and mull over the following:

Are there any potential unintended consequences here that I've not considered?

Is there anyone I should consult before acting unilaterally?

Will this decision increase my team's freedom to do its work, or decrease it? If the answer is "decrease," are there any changes I can make to lessen the pain?

Many leaders don't take the time to think in this way, and the (unintended) result is that the team gets batted around like a pinball rather than actually making progress on the Work.

I recommend that you write this sentence on an index card and keep it on your wall or desk: "How will this affect the Work?" It will remind you that every decision and demand you make now has a long lever attached to it, and the unintended consequences could affect a lot of people. (If you'd like a downloadable/printable version of this, go to toddhenry.com/thework.)

The road you travel from control to influence will probably be a bumpy one. However, as you begin to see your influence scale throughout the organization, and as you see the unique abilities of the people on your team come alive, that's when leadership gets really fun. The transition to influence and total accountability requires patience, faith, and a willingness to live in the tension.

CHECKPOINT

You own it all! There is no place left to point a finger. Lead by influence and define the playing field for your team so that team members feel the freedom they need to do their best work.

Actions

—Begin to establish your principles and leadership philosophy. Take thirty minutes in the next week to write down a list of tenets that provide rails within which your team will operate. At the very least, they should include (a) what kinds of behavior you will celebrate, (b) the rules of team engagement, (c) how you determine priorities in doing the work, and (d) how you determine whether the work is good or bad.

—Write "How will this affect the Work?" on an index card and place it in a prominent place in your workspace.

Conversations

Ask your team members, in group format or individually, the following questions:

—Am I doing anything that's preventing you from having the freedom you need to do your job?

—What can I do to better equip you for success? Do you feel like you have the space, focus, time, and resources you need?

Rituals

These rituals are also collected at the end of the book under weekly, monthly, and quarterly categories so that you can engage in them regularly.

Weekly: Do a quick scan of your principles or leadership philosophy and consider any areas where you or the team might be violating them.

Monthly: Spend some time considering the marks of good leadership. (For example, from chapter 1: *a good leader of creative people accomplishes the objectives while developing the team's ability to shoulder new and more challenging work.*) Do you feel like you are accomplishing these right now, or is there an area you need to work on?

Quarterly: Review your guiding principles to make sure that they are still relevant and comprehensive.

CHAPTER 4

LEVEL UP

The Shift from Equals to Imbalance

Nearly all men can stand adversity, but if you want to test a man's character, give him power.

—Abraham Lincoln

PRINCIPLE: To create stability, you need to distance yourself (a bit) from your team.

The workplace is unfair. Although we love the idea that we exist in a meritocracy, where the best ideas win the day, the reality is that it's impossible to parse why some average people or ideas rise to the top and other, more deserving ones are ignored.

That's why, when leading creative work, the team's perception of your objectivity is important. They need to know that you are able to consider ideas and potential directions for the work without being clouded by personal relationships or the persuasiveness of a particular team member. If your team loses its trust in your objectivity, your credibility suffers. However, maintaining objectivity is tricky because you have existing relationships with team members, and those relationships (to some extent) probably extend beyond the workplace.

It's your responsibility to establish boundaries in your work relationships. Healthy and clear boundaries help keep potential conflicts of interest at bay and ensure that your team feels completely secure in how and why decisions get made. An old saying argues that "good fences make good neighbors," and the same principle applies here. When you assume a leadership role, you need to redefine your relationships with team members, not only for *your* sake but also for *theirs*.

BLINDSIDED BY POWER

Ever heard the old warning "Be careful what you wish for, because you just might get it"?

That was how Ken felt at the end of his first day in his new role. Over the past year, he had worked hard to separate himself from his peers by excelling at every project he was handed. He not only did everything he was asked to do, but he was always seeking additional responsibility to prove that he was a team player. He was a rising star. His internal reviews were off the charts, and it was clear that he was gunning to move up through the ranks as quickly as he could. Finally, his manager was moved into a different role, and Ken was in turn promoted to team leader. Now all of his peers reported to him, and for the first time Ken really took stock of his situation: the day before they had all been coworkers, and now Ken was their boss.

Aside from the barely veiled jealousy from peers who thought they deserved the role, which he expected, Ken also sensed that his team members, even some former peers with whom he'd worked very closely, were more guarded around him. Over the coming weeks, it became clear that his relationships were never returning to what they'd been before his promotion. Worse, Ken was uncertain that the additional responsibility was even worth what he'd lost. He was happy with the raise, and he knew that his work would be different, but he didn't realize how much his relationships would change once he was in a position of authority over his former peers.

Another creative director told me over coffee that his entire team had recently decided to go out for a happy hour celebration after a grueling project. Unfortunately, he only found out as photos started showing up on social media. Although he has a great relationship with the team, he told me that he realized in that moment, as he was sitting at home scrolling through those images, that as much as he wants to be buddies with everyone on the team, it will never happen. They see him as different, or set apart.

People in a new leadership role are often caught off guard by how much the relational dynamics change. Once you are in a position of authority, people will treat you differently, whether consciously or not. They are likely to filter most interactions they have with you through the lens of how it affects their jobs.

For people in creative roles, any ambiguity about how decisions will get made—how your whims and wishes might affect their jobs and how their relationship with you has changed along with your new role—is nothing but a distraction from their core work. When you make an effort to clarify those areas of confusion, it helps them to focus their brainpower on more important matters.

Power changes the dynamics of relationships forever. However, that doesn't have to be a bad thing. It all depends on how you manage the transition from equals to imbalance.

There are two things that you must do in order to set healthy boundaries and manage the power dynamic effectively: establish distance and put your gun away.

ESTABLISH (A LITTLE) DISTANCE

Your responsibility to the organization means that you must do what's in the best interest of the team, even if it's at the expense of your friendships. You will have to make tough calls about who gets to work on prestigious projects, who gets promoted, and at times, unfortunately, who needs to be fired. Ideally, you'll have an expectations-clarifying conversation with each team member very early in your new role so that you can set boundaries and show that you've thought through how you'll handle conflicts between your work position and your personal relationships when they inevitably arise. In my experience, few leaders do this.

Is this *really* necessary? Shouldn't adults be able to handle a leadership transition like this without jumping through hoops? Probably. Yet human behavior is complicated, and emotions are unpredictable.

Rob Rivenburgh is CEO, North America, for the Mars Agency, but prior to this role he had filled leadership roles on both the agency and client side in multiple industries. In one of those early roles, he made the mistake of not establishing enough distance between himself and his team when he was promoted. There were many awkward situations in which his (still) close relationships with former peers made it difficult to make decisions that he knew would affect their careers, such as how high-profile work was distributed or who had to work on the weekend, even when he knew what was best for both them and the company. "It led to a lot of hurt feelings and blurry lines," he said.

When you fail to have conversations to establish new and clear boundaries with your former peers, it will inevitably affect their willingness to trust you. However, if you have an intentional conversation about this early and deliberately, it can actually *improve* the trust of your team members. They will see that you also recognize the awkwardness of the situation and want to clarify and simplify expectations.

"It's really about self-awareness," Rivenburgh continued. "You have to understand that others view you differently when you are the leader."

These are never easy conversations, but they are much easier than dealing with months of relational ambiguity or suddenly having to make a difficult decision because you hadn't discussed expectations and boundaries. Your conversations about boundaries should happen before they become urgent. Plan how you want to approach your team members—especially those you were close to prior to your new position—because each conversation will require a different touch. The conversations should have three elements, in this order: (1) What has changed? (2) What's the same? and (3) What can I do for you?

When you fail to establish new and clear boundaries with your former peers, it will inevitably affect their willingness to trust you.

What has changed? Address the eight-hundred-pound gorilla in the room. The first thing to talk about is the behaviors you can no longer engage in. These behaviors might include long, casual conversations during the workday, social routines like having lunch together every day, or conversations (gossip) about fellow team members.

Kevin was promoted to lead his former peers and failed to have this conversation. Every day, Mark would stop by Kevin's new desk to shoot the breeze, talking about a ball game or what's happening that weekend or something else equally irrelevant to the work they were doing. In the old days, Mark and Kevin shared a workspace, and they would sometimes engage in this kind of banter to kill time before a meeting or in those last few minutes at the end of the day, but now it was an awkward and unwelcome distraction to Kevin. However, he didn't want it to seem like his promotion had gone to his head, so he let it carry on way too long, until he finally had to tell Mark that it needed to end, which to Mark likely felt like a slap in the face and a betrayal of their friendship. If Kevin had simply said, "Listen, Mark. I've really enjoyed our conversations in the middle of the workday, and I'd love for them to continue, but we're going to need to find time for it because my responsibilities have changed." He could have offered a few solutions, like walking to lunch a few days a week or taking a coffee break or something that would have prevented the inevitable awkwardness.

At the same time, it's important to call out what your new responsibilities mean about how you must approach your relationships. Because of your new role, you have to hold your former coworkers accountable for showing up on time, putting the proper level of thought into their work, and working well with peers.

What's the same? It's also important to recognize what's not changed about the relational dynamic. Your promotion doesn't mean that you can't be friends or that you can't go to lunch or spend time together. Make sure that you communicate clearly what you hope your relationship will look like going forward. For example, "I really hope we can continue to play tennis a few times a week," or "I'd still love to go to happy hour with our group when your schedule allows."

Just because you're now in a position of authority doesn't mean that you need to abandon your friendships or cut off all social ties to your team. However, it's important that you express what you hope the relationship will look like so that you relieve their uncertainty. You also must be careful not to create a perception of favoritism or inappropriate behavior. Reinforce your perception of the relationship and the ways you hope you will continue to connect and share ideas.

What can I do for you? A great way to end the conversation about new boundaries is by offering your help. Now that you are in a position of leadership, make sure that the people on your team know that you are committed to serving them and helping them accomplish their goals. This is a great time to show them that you're serious about *their* success. Some questions you might ask include:

Is there anything you need that you don't have?

Is there any way in which I can better set you up for your work?

Do you need more clarity about anything we're doing right now?

Are you struggling with anything I don't know about? Can I help?

Also, this is a good time to reinforce the specific qualities that you see in them and that you're committed to helping them bring these qualities to the team. Show them that you recognize that your success as a leader is dependent upon their success as team members.

QUIT YOUR APPROVAL ADDICTION

Everyone wants to be liked. Given the choice between being liked or disliked, no one chooses the latter. In fact, for some leaders I've met, being liked is at the top of their list of priorities. They wouldn't admit it, but their actions prove otherwise. They avoid any form of conflict, fail to speak truth, and generally blend in with the majority crowd whenever possible.

However, they often do so at the expense of their effectiveness as a leader. They crave perception over progress.

In a former professional life, Jim Friedman was an Emmy Award–winning TV producer and writer, but these days he is an acclaimed professor in the Institute of Entrepreneurship at Miami University in Oxford, Ohio. He believes that one of the biggest mistakes leaders make is trying to be liked. "However, it's not my job to be liked," he told me. "It's my job to help them do their best work." In reality, Friedman is a massively popular professor, but one of the reasons that he sometimes overhears students speaking about him unfavorably or is the target of frustration during office hours is his willingness to speak the plain truth. His directness sometimes feels abrasive to students, even when it's the exact thing they need in order to grow. (This strategy has obviously worked well for Friedman, as he was recently voted Miami University's Professor of the Year.)

If you tend to be a people pleaser, it is possible to flip the script, but it doesn't mean being a dislikable SOB. Rather, it means speaking truth to people in a way they can hear it. Here are a few strategies to help you unplug from your approval addiction.

Speak truth with empathy. You can be a truth teller and do it in a way that others are likely to receive it well. Whenever you have to deliver difficult truth to someone, consider the context, the timing, and how the other person is most likely to positively receive your words. Don't tack it on at the end of a meeting or when you're about to rush out the door to another commitment. (I offer more tips for communicating with empathy in *Louder Than Words*.) *Where in your work/life are you shying away from speaking truth because you prefer to be liked?*

Refuse to throw a team member under the bus. When others are gossiping about a coworker or assigning blame for something, it's tempting to jump into the conversation in order to feel included and be liked. However, each time you engage in one of these conversations, you are creating a little breach in trust. Your team members never know when they might be the subject of your ridicule. Never throw someone under the bus, even if it's deserved. *Are there situations in which you know these conversations are likely to happen, and can you avoid them?*

Maintain your edge. Over time, it's easy to allow organizational life to soften your point of view. You may adopt a milder demeanor so that you fit in better, but doing so causes you to lose your strong competitive and creative advantage. Don't feel the need to alter your perspective out of a desire to play organizational politics in order to be liked. The edge that people scoff at now is the very thing they will celebrate later. The opinions you hold (that few others do) and the quirky but incisive insights that you bring to the table are likely to be your calling card in years to come. That's the stuff of great leadership. *Where are you compromising your perspective and softening your edge in order to be liked?*

When you arrive at a decision or are facing a crossroads with a project, ask, "Am I doing this to be liked or to be effective?" This is one of the most difficult traps to avoid, and it is why leadership is often described as being lonely.

Remember, you *can* be both liked and effective, but you *can't* chase both at the same time. When you are genuinely leading your team from a place of empathy—of caring deeply about *their* ambitions and growth—they will begin to sense that even your most direct and painful feedback is in their best interest. However, when you soften your feedback to be liked, you are serving neither yourself nor the team. And the work will suffer too.

Also, remember that as you distance yourself from the team and create boundaries, not everyone will approve. Leadership is like living in a fishbowl in the middle of a shooting range. Everyone can see what you're doing, and they may feel free to take shots at you whenever they like. You'll be judged for what you do and what you don't do, for things you say (that you don't even remember or didn't mean), and for things you were never a part of (but somehow you have been placed at the scene of the crime). It's human nature for people to look for someone to blame when things don't go as expected, and as the leader you will be in the crosshairs. It's not fair, especially when you've done everything you can to do right by your team; but it's reality.

Make peace with the fact that when you step into leadership, you forfeit your right to a fair trial. Typically, you will have access to more information than the people you lead and, thus, have greater perspective on why certain decisions are being made. They won't understand, and you won't be able to explain. If you're driven by a need to be liked, then you'll spend every waking hour playing whack-a-mole with the unfair assumptions of others.

You *can* be both liked and effective, but you *can't* chase both at the same time.

So get used to having a target on your back, because people need someone to blame when things go wrong. However, just because others are taking shots at you doesn't mean that you should shoot back. In fact, you should do the opposite.

PUT YOUR GUN AWAY

Imagine that we're having a disagreement over where to go to lunch.

"You know," I plead, "I've been craving pasta all week."

"Yeah," you might reply, "but I'm really in the mood for Mexican."

The argument might continue until we reach a compromise or one of us finally wins over the other. Simple enough.

Now imagine that same conversation, only this time I'm casually waving a loaded gun in your direction while arguing for the Italian restaurant down the block.

"I have to say, I've been craving pasta all week."

"OK," you reply. "Whatever you want."

You may be *really* craving a burrito, but you've lost your will to argue. Obviously, the loaded gun changes the power dynamic in the conversation and makes your personal survival more important than what's on the menu for lunch. (And, needless to say, I've probably lost my lunch partner.)

We are wired to value survival over comfort (rightly so!), so we'll compromise personal preference if we believe our life is threatened. This is not only true in literal life-or-death scenarios, but it's also the case when our livelihood is in danger. When someone believes that her job is at risk, she starts to second-guess whether it's worth it to dissent.

As the leader of the team, you're holding the loaded gun. Your team recognizes that you have the ability to make its work life either amazing or miserable. If you are not careful with how you wield your authority, you can easily squelch team members' willingness to speak their minds during disagreements or to share ideas that might seem unsafe. This means they might leave their most creative work on the table.

What is your first response when a team member challenges an idea you've introduced? Is it *POW! POW!* straight in their direction? Do you shoot first and ask questions later? If you get defensive and wield your power to protect your ego and your position, then you will eventually train everyone around you not to share uncomfortable thoughts. Instead, they will quietly acquiesce and let you have your way, because you hold the power.

Put away your loaded gun. Create an environment in which people feel comfortable introducing ideas that challenge the status quo, respectfully disagreeing with your opinions and pointing out inconvenient truths. No one wins when teams choose to bury these alternative viewpoints. Besides, everyone knows what's really going on, even if no one is talking about it.

As the leader of the team, you're holding the loaded gun. . . . Put away your loaded gun.

No matter how many times you tell them it's OK to speak up, they won't do so until you prove it with your actions. You might be thinking, *But wait! I'm the most open-minded, considerate leader I know!* That could be true, but there are subtle ways in which you might be trigger-happy.

Getting defensive when someone offers feedback. Do you feel the need to power up every time someone disagrees with you or offers disconfirming information? These power plays aren't typically obvious but include subtle hints of your position or importance within the organization. You might rationalize your actions to others by pointing out that they don't have the same information that you do, or that you have more experience. You might patronize them and pretend to be listening while sending them subtle signals that you don't respect their opinion.

Making threats when you're not willing to follow through. The other day, on a quick trip to the grocery store, I noticed a little boy running around the produce section and knocking items off the stands. His mother turned around and called him. "Joshua, you put that down and come here. Joshua! OK—I'm counting to three, then you're going to be in trouble—one, two, THREE! Joshua, I mean it this time—you're going to go in time-out! One, two, [long and frustrated pause] THREE!" Then, when Joshua didn't respond, she walked over and took him by the hand, put him in the cart, and handed him a phone to keep him entertained.

Having parented three toddlers, I understand the frustration and occasional futility of trying to corral a kid in a public space. At the same time, continual threats of punishment without follow-through do more harm than good.

Although leading adults is obviously a little more nuanced than parenting a child, the principle holds. Making veiled threats is like waving a loaded gun that you never intend to use. Your team will stop listening to you.

Hoarding important information. Some people are more passive-aggressive in how they abuse their power. They might choose to withhold important information in order to prove their importance to the organization. They constantly remind everyone around them how "there's more to this, but I can't talk about it right now," but "in a week or so I'll tell you why we're doing all of this." It's really nothing more than a way for them to show that they are in a position of power and that everyone else is more out of the loop than they are. Sure, there will always be information that's not appropriate to share with the team, but constantly reminding everyone can sometimes seem like a power play. It only creates anxiety and dissonance. Don't use the unknown as an instrument of power.

The transition from equals to an imbalance in power is often challenging for leaders in new roles. Have transparent conversations early about how things have changed. Put aside your need to be liked and put your gun away so that you can have straightforward conversations with your team about your expectations, without any hidden agendas or unnecessary power plays. Doing so will earn the trust of your team and set it up to introduce new ideas without the fear of politics or a personal relationship getting in the way of success.

CHECKPOINT

Your team is not a family. Make sure that you set appropriate boundaries while also striving to maintain your relationships. Here are a few ways to do so:

Actions

—Identify a relationship with a team member in which the boundaries are unclear, then have a clarifying conversation.

—Note a situation, whether a specific team meeting or a one-on-one, when you tend to get defensive when challenged. Instead, put your gun away and listen intently to the feedback.

Conversations

Have a conversation with key team members about the following:

—Is there any situation or project where you wish I'd listen better to your ideas or opinions?

—What can I do to set you up for success in your role?

Rituals

These rituals are also collected at the end of the book under weekly, monthly, and quarterly categories so that you can engage in them regularly.

Weekly: As you look at your upcoming schedule, consider any meetings or situations where you might encounter a power imbalance. How will you make everyone involved feel engaged and welcome to bring their best ideas? (This could mean having conversations ahead of time to encourage people to speak or being extra careful to put your gun away during the meeting.)

Monthly: Invite someone on your team to connect with you over lunch or coffee with the sole purpose of getting to know the person better and understand his or her aspirations.

Quarterly: Do a broad review of your relationships on your team and note any relational awkwardness or power imbalances that have developed.

CHAPTER 5

LEAD BRILLIANCE

The Shift from Peer to Coach

A leader takes people where they want to go. A great leader takes people where they don't necessarily want to go, but ought to be.

—Rosalynn Carter

PRINCIPLE: To challenge your team, you need to help people see those aspects of their abilities to which they are blind.

When I was a kid, my father stepped in to coach my junior high basketball team when it was obvious that we hadn't the slightest clue what we were doing. (I'm not exaggerating. If we took a shot and hit the rim during a game, the stands would erupt in applause. We lost one game 49–2.)

It was never easy being the coach's son, because I had to balance two relationships with the same person. First and foremost, he was my dad. At home, I could complain about smack-talking team members and have a personal conversation about my frustrations. However, once practice started, he was my coach. One time at practice, I passed up an open shot because I didn't want my friends thinking my dad was favoring me by letting me shoot too much. It quickly became apparent that he wasn't when he laid into me in front of the entire team. In that moment, I realized that my dad was also managing two relationships: he was my dad, but he was also responsible for helping the team be the best it could be. This meant that it was more important to do what was right for the team *and* me, even if that meant doing something that went against his instincts as a father. (Needless to say, I didn't pass up any open shots the rest of the season.)

Every brilliant creative pro needs a coach to help them unleash their potential. There are a number of things that talented people *can* do, but there is a limited amount of focus and time in which to do them. And similar to the example above, you must play dual roles for your team members: you must help them become the best they can be individually while also helping them understand and accept their role within the overall team.

PUT 'EM IN, COACH

A good coach helps a creative person identify her strengths, focus on areas where she can achieve unique and valuable impact, and keep moving forward after she fails. The best thing that a coach can do is keep a creative person out of his own head so that he doesn't get stuck ruminating on his fears of what might go wrong. Instead, a coach helps them focus on possibilities.

Although responsible for the ultimate results, a great athletic coach doesn't go out onto the court (or field), grab the ball, and start playing the game for the team. She also doesn't constantly yell instructions at the team during a game, to the point that the team loses all sense of what's important and what's not. No, a great coach understands that the most important instruction comes during practice, when there is time to have intentional conversations about what's working and what's not, and when the pressure isn't boiling over. She also knows that to perform well as a team, each member must understand her role and play it well. Naturally, these same considerations apply to your work team.

Michael Bungay Stanier is the founder of the company Box of Crayons. He spends much of his time helping organizational leaders learn how to coach well. In his book *The Coaching Habit*, he argues that "coaching should be a daily, informal act, not an occasional, formal 'It's Coaching Time!' event." This means that regular, informal conversation about how things are going is critical if you want to help others unleash their best work. It also means that as a leader you need to spend much of your time thinking about the people on your team, considering how you might be able to help them go to the next level.

It's tempting to just drop advice on another person because you probably have the experience and perspective to be able to see what's best for her. (It's also less emotionally taxing than engaging in a long conversation.) However, insights are much more powerful if your team member arrives at them on her own. Stanier told me, "If you shift to question asking, you are giving the other person the chance to define the conversation."

A young woman named Suzanne told me that she struggled with poor coaching from a manager early in her career. She loved her role, which allowed her to engage in work that she knew was making a difference, but her manager felt the need to tell her at every turn what she needed to do next. She told me she felt like she was suffocating. When she came to him with a question, he would just give advice and send her off, but there was no conversation about why it was good advice. This is typical behavior in many organizations I encounter, and although it's very efficient for the leader in the short run, it's very counterproductive in the long run. In these situations, you are not coaching; you are commanding. It's like you're playing the game for them.

A friend listens to you, then offers advice. A coach sets the stage and helps you arrive at the answer yourself. Although there are many roles that a coach can play, when leading creative people there are two primary coaching roles to master: helping them understand what *truly* drives them, and helping them perform at their full potential.

HELP THEM UNDERSTAND WHAT DRIVES THEM

Creative people often have broad shoulders and diverse capabilities. There are a lot of things the people on your team *could* do. The question is, *should* they? If you put someone in a position where every day of work feels like drudgery, he might succeed for a while, but his motivation will wane over time, and he will struggle with burnout and dissatisfaction. As we saw in chapter 2, people grow bored if they do not feel appropriately challenged. Being in a role that pushes people to grow can make the difference between passable work and *exceptional* work.

As a coach, it's your job to help the talented, creative people discover the work they are *made* for and that lights their fire. This doesn't mean that they will love every task they do—no one does—but it does mean that they are generally doing work that gives them a sense of engagement and gratification. Executive recruiter David Wiser

A friend listens to you, then offers advice. A coach sets the stage and helps you arrive at the answer yourself.

told me, "Just because they have the experience and skills to do the work doesn't mean they are right for a particular job. They will get bored very quickly if they are not in the right place, and that will create problems for everyone." Wiser categorizes most jobs into one of three categories: jobs for *builders*, jobs for *fixers*, and jobs for *optimizers*.

Builders are people who live for the process of creating something new. They want a clean slate, a difficult problem to solve, and no instruction manual. They thrive on ideas and the chaos of early-stage projects, and they are at their best when they are figuring things out as they go. However, when you ask a builder to work on a more mature project or to manage something already in progress, they will drive you crazy. They are perpetually seeking a way to blow things up and start over. They will try to split off the project and create something new. They are not satisfied with tweaking something that's already there—they always have to be innovating.

Fixers are people who get charged up by analysis and diagnosis. They can quickly scan a situation, identify the broken dynamics, and find a solution. They are always in search of a broken system, and they are most motivated when they feel needed to fix a specific problem. A fixer can't listen to a conversation without stepping in to offer advice and can't tolerate open loops. However, if you assign a fixer to a brand-new project with no parameters, they will often become paralyzed. They are great at problem solving, but they don't always do well with few parameters.

Optimizers are people who get excited about taking something good and making it great. They are tweakers by nature. They are always looking for efficiencies and hate to see waste. They make the meetings more efficient, the workflow more productive, and the team more focused and lean. They often lack tolerance for the inefficiency of creative work and the uncertainty of entrepreneurship. They do best in roles where they have clearly defined objectives and ways to quantify their performance.

If you are launching a brand-new project with few rails and a lot of exploratory work to do, you probably don't want an optimizer leading the charge. If you are trying to get to the bottom of why your clients seem unsatisfied with their interactions with your team, you probably don't want a builder on the job. Understanding the natural motivational archetype of your team members, and their "sweet spot" of engagement, is critical not only to set them up for success, but also helps them feel engaged and motivated to bring their best.

As a coach, you are responsible for helping people understand their sweet spot of motivation and effectiveness. If you don't, you will be drawing water from a shallow well. However, if you do, they will bring their heart and soul to their job. Although no one gets to operate exclusively in their sweet spot, the more your team does, the better it will function and the less friction you'll experience. For your team, consider the following:

Who are your builders? These are the people who come alive in group brainstorms or at the beginning of a new client initiative and who will stay late into the night working on the early stages of a project, but they have to drag themselves to meetings about the final deliverables. How can you better set them up to do work in which they are creating value in white spaces and establishing new trails for the team to follow? Or, can you give them a handful of "skunk works," projects to play with that will be both challenging and fulfilling and that might create long-term value for the organization? These are back-burner, speculative projects that they can play around on and use their entrepreneurial skills to build in a low-pressure, low-risk way. If you don't find a way to keep your builders challenged and motivated, you may find them trying to blow things up to start fresh, even when things are working just fine.

Who are your fixers? How can you help them connect with problems that are valuable to the organization but have a clear and specified end point? (You don't want fixers working on never-ending problems—they will get bored and eventually generate unnecessary complexity.) The best opportunities for fixers are those pain points that no one else seems to have the time or the energy to address but are impeding the progress of the team.

Who are your optimizers? They might be constantly tweaking systems and workflows to make them better, from their meeting schedules to the technology they are using to accomplish their work. Identify these optimizers and help them align around inefficient processes or areas of organizational misalignment that could use their help.

Now, as you consider the team's current workload, *how much of its portfolio of responsibilities is consistent with each team member's natural motivational archetype?* How much time and energy do people spend on activities that run counter to the kind of work that naturally fuels their fire? This is a good coaching discussion to have with each team member—as a way to help people discover where they feel stuck, where they're bored with the work, and where they have opportunity to grow.

Is there a way in which you could modify the workload so that each team member is operating more in his or her sweet spot? Are there tasks that could be off-loaded to people who are more naturally motivated to do them? Do you need to shift the balance of the team's workload to position your team members for greater success?

Now, as a leader, consider the following questions for yourself:

Are you more naturally a builder, a fixer, or an optimizer? Which kind of activity do you find naturally motivating and are drawn to when you have discretion over your activities? When you approach a problem, which is your default response?

How much of your current workload is in your sweet spot, and how much focus, time, and energy do you spend doing things that are difficult for you to get excited about? As pros, from time to time we all have to do work that we'd prefer not to, but there is little use in swimming upstream your entire career when no one is asking you to. Is your current role built around your core motivational archetype, or do you spend most of your time doing things that are far outside what you're wired for? If work is drudgery for you, it will be difficult for you to light the team's fire.

Is there an easy way for you to rebalance some of your portfolio so that you're operating more consistently in your natural motivational archetype? This might mean finding others who are naturally drawn to those activities and handing them off. If you're a natural builder, find an optimizer to tackle the refinement of systems or restructuring of the organization. If you're a natural optimizer, you might want to find someone else to help you with "blue sky" initiatives, at least until things are more framed up for you.

COACHING YOUR TEAM UP TO ITS POTENTIAL

Employee disengagement is a topic of intense interest for many organizations, and for good reason. A 2015 study by Gallup found that 51 percent of American workers were "not engaged" on the job, and an additional 17.5 percent were "actively disengaged." That means that a mere 31.5 percent of people surveyed felt engaged on a daily basis. That's a staggering amount of untapped potential and a depressing statement about how many workers consider their work to be a necessary evil, not a pathway to satisfaction and growth. (Perhaps the saddest part is that the percentage of engaged workers is the highest it's been since Gallup began doing the study in 2000.) The good news is that, as a leader, you have the ability to shatter these norms for your team.

Scott Mautz has held many leadership positions over the course of his career, most recently as the leader of a $3 billion business division at Procter & Gamble, and he now runs his own training firm. He believes that engaged, fully invested team members rarely result from typical motivational tactics like pay and title. To Mautz, it's more about cultivating a culture of discovery. "When people work with a sense of discovery it's incredibly powerful. . . . You have to grant people a sense that they are on a journey of growth in their work."

As the coach, cultivate a sense of discovery and growth on your team. Allow people the opportunity to try new things, to learn from their mistakes, and to identify limiting beliefs.

Allow cross-functional experimentation. Do your team members ever have the opportunity to experiment with different kinds of work or take on responsibilities that aren't core to their job description? This doesn't mean that you should toss people into the deep end, of course, or compromise the work of the team just to allow someone to try something new, but you should allow people the opportunity to push themselves and develop new skills that will reinforce the team's resilience.

Jeremy Bailey, creative director at the cloud accounting software company FreshBooks, told me about a practice that involves what he calls circles, or "specialized groups of people who add value to the rest of the organization." These people provide their unique skills to parts of the organization in which they normally don't work, which "keeps them out of ruts." Bailey said, "Even though it's extracurricular, it has become one of the most important growth opportunities for our team."

Are there ways you could help your team members step outside their normal routines and ruts and grow their skills? To assess how ready they are for such a change, here are a few coaching questions you can ask:

How challenged by your work do you feel right now? What do you think might help you increase your sense of challenge?

Is there any work that you wish you could do but that isn't a part of your normal workload? Why?

Are there any skills that you've always wanted to develop but don't have the chance to in the course of your normal work?

When do you feel most engaged in your work, and why? How can I help you do more of that kind of work?

Remember that these conversations are about helping people come to their own conclusions, with perspective and guidance from you.

When they fail, take a pause. After a failed project, many teams simply move forward to the next one, without a postmortem. This is a huge mistake. It's important that you seize those failures and mistakes and turn them into growth moments for your team. Otherwise, people are likely to commit the same mistakes again. Some of the biggest coaching opportunities you'll have are in the moments when an individual or the team has failed.

Mike Krzyzewski, the legendary head basketball coach for Duke University, said in an interview: "My defining moments have usually been something where I've lost or where I've been knocked back." At the end of the 1983 season, Duke lost by 43 in the ACC tournament. The program was in disarray and many thought that Coach K's career was over. At dinner that night, someone raised his glass and said, "Here's to forgetting about tonight." Coach K stopped him and ordered him to put his glass down. Then he raised his own glass and said, "Here's to *never* forgetting about tonight."

The following season, when the team arrived on October 15 for the first practice, the scoreboard over the court read 109–66, the final score of the tournament loss to Virginia. Players recounted that Coach K wanted them to never forget how it felt to get beat so thoroughly and to use it as fuel to give their best every day. Since that day, Duke has emerged as a premier basketball program, and Coach K largely points to that defining moment as the turning point.

Here are a few questions to ask shortly after experiencing a failure. It's very important that you couch this conversation as a desire to learn from the experience and grow, not as a trial of competence:

Why do you think you/we fell short of our objectives?

What did you learn from this experience? What will you do differently next time?

Was the failure one of effort, decision making, or skill? How can you avoid it again? (By the way, failures of effort require special treatment, because it's the one kind of failure that is completely avoidable.)

If you were me, what would you do to prevent these mistakes in the future?

Avoid the temptation to backward rationalize poor results as acceptable; instead, highlight them and use them as fuel for improvement. **Help them uncover their inner narratives.** Finally, make every effort to identify narratives that your team members have adopted that limit their ability to bring their best. These can be negative narratives, such as false beliefs about their lack of ability or level of permission to speak or act, or they can be an inflated sense of capability that needs to be brought back down to earth. No one benefits when a team member is living with an artificially curbed or inflated sense of their abilities. Once those limiting beliefs are out in the open, watch for them and coach team members past the obstacles when they begin to affect their work behavior.

Here are a few questions to ask to help you identify these beliefs:

What do you see as your greatest contribution to the team right now?

What do you think is holding you back the most in your effort to do great work?

If you could change one thing about your current skill set, what would it be?

These are just door-opening questions. Remember to listen more than your speak. This is not about your tossing wisdom nuggets at your grateful team member; it's about your listening to their needs and perceptions and helping them arrive at a greater sense of their potential. Scott Mautz told me, "You need to practice the WAIT principle: 'Why Am I Talking?'

Avoid the temptation to backward rationalize poor results as acceptable; instead, highlight them and use them as fuel for improvement.

Whenever you are engaged with a team member, spend far more time asking questions and listening than you do talking."

COACH THE *WHY*, NOT JUST THE *WHAT*

I once heard a story of a family gathered for a Saturday evening dinner. The two adult children had agreed to make dinner for the entire extended family, and as they got ready to put a ham into the oven, one of the siblings cut off both ends of the ham and placed it in a pan. Perplexed, the other sibling asked why he had cut them off, and thus wasted a significant portion of a perfectly good ham. He didn't know why, but their mother always did it as well. And when they asked her, she said that she had picked up the habit from her own mother. Finally, the curiosity got the best of all of them, and they asked their grandmother:

"Oh, that's easy," Grandma replied. "When your grandpa and I were first married, we didn't have much money, but we were given some cooking ware by a family friend. Unfortunately, the pan I used for baking was too small for an entire ham, so I had to cut the ends off to make it fit in the pan before I could bake it."

A desperate, innovative act became a multigenerational tradition (and resulted in a lot of wasted ham!) because no one ever thought to ask *why*. In the same way, your team can easily adopt rote behavior without ever truly understanding the *why* behind that behavior. When asked, they might respond, "That's the way we've always done it." They may even accomplish a lot using these rote systems, but when a new and unfamiliar challenge arises, they won't be able to adapt their methods because they don't understand why they work in the first place. A big part of your coaching role is to help your team understand not only what works, but also why you are doing it that way and why it works.

In his book *How the Mighty Fall*, researcher Jim Collins argues that one of the key signs of the decline of a once-great organization is when its employees exhibit an understanding of what works but have no clue *why* it works. Even with this gap, they can continue to produce results for a season, but they will eventually falter once circumstances change, and the old methods are no longer effective. It's possible to understand the tactics that have led to past success but still have no clue why those tactics succeeded. Coach the *why*.

Are you just coaching your team members about what to do, or are you teaching them *why* it works? This simple tweak can make a huge difference in their growth and development and can also help your team scale in capacity much more quickly. Here are a few ways to do it:

Have group "why chats" about big decisions. Whenever you are announcing a key decision in a team meeting or are implementing a new way of doing things, have an open discussion about why it's happening. As tempting as it may be to try to justify the decision out of the gate, try instead to encourage a discussion about why team members think this is (or isn't) the right direction. Ask them what they would do in your situation. See if you can help them understand the complexity of the problem and why you believe that the decision you've made is the right one.

Coach them on the why *behind your decisions and methods.* Don't just teach tactics, explain why they work. Train your people to be adaptive so that they aren't reliant on you. This is what a great coach does.

Great creative leaders are committed to helping their team members discover and understand their strengths and motivations on their own and then position themselves so that they're taking full advantage of them.

> **It's possible to understand the tactics that have led to past success but still have no clue why those tactics succeeded. Coach the *why*.**

Don't be a passive manager; be an active coach. Get to know your team, listen well, help people *own* their work, and commit yourself to their growth. They will reward you with unique, brilliant ideas and deep commitment to you and the work.

CHECKPOINT

A friend will listen to you and encourage you, but a coach knows when to challenge you to do better. Commit to pushing your team to go beyond its perceived limits. Here are a few ways to do so:

Actions

—Identify the builders, the fixers, and the optimizers on your team.

—Have one-on-one conversations with team members about their level of enthusiasm for their current workload and how you might help them better align their core motivations with their workload.

—Have a "why chat" about a big decision that's been made or a process that seems too opaque. Make sure everyone understands not just *what* it is, but *why* it works.

Conversations

Have a conversation with key team members about the following:

—Do you feel challenged by your work right now? What might help you increase your sense of challenge and engagement?

—Is there any work that you wish you could do but that isn't a part of your normal workload? Why?

Rituals

These rituals are also collected at the end of the book under weekly, monthly, and quarterly categories so that you can engage in them regularly.

Weekly: Schedule a one-on-one coaching meeting with at least one person on your team this week. Listen to them and help them identify areas for growth.

Monthly: Consider someplace where your team has fallen short of its objectives. Schedule a time to discuss the failure and what you learned from it. Don't make this intimidating; make the conversation casual, and ensure that your team knows that there won't be any yelling or blaming. It's for learning purposes only.

Quarterly: Consider the rhythm of your coaching conversations and your team's response to them. Have you seen growth in your team over the past few months? If not, how do you need to challenge individual team members to step out of their comfort zone?

PART TWO

YOUR MECHANICS

CHAPTER 6

EARN THE RIGHT

Managing Trust

A leader is best when people barely know he exists; when his work is done, his aim fulfilled, they will say: we did it ourselves.

—Lao-tzu

PRINCIPLE: To provide stability, you must earn, manage, and strive to maintain your team's trust.

Imagine that you're driving down an unfamiliar country road. It's a beautiful day, the sun is shining, and you see nothing but straightaway ahead of you, stretching off into the distance. Until, that is, you come to a road sign saying there's a gradual right curve ahead, over the next hill, with a speed limit of forty-five miles per hour.

No problem, you think. *I can probably actually take that curve at fifty miles per hour. They always exaggerate the speed limit.* However, as you approach the blind curve, another sign suddenly appears that indicates that it's *not*, in fact, a right curve, but a left one, and that it's shaped more like a hairpin, with a speed limit of fifteen miles per hour. You slam on the brakes and hope that you can make the curve and avoid the ditch.

Now let's say that you're successful in avoiding an accident. What do you think will happen the next time you see a sign indicating there's a gradual curve ahead, over the next hill? Will you trust the sign implicitly, or will you slow down to a crawl and scope out the curve yourself? If you're like me, you'd probably need a little more firsthand proof of the *actual* road conditions before staking your life.

In creative work, everything hinges on trust. You establish a direction and your team pours itself—its time, energy, heart, passion—into the work. They can't always see over the next hill, so you are planting the road signs and giving them a sense of what's ahead. They need to know that their efforts are not in vain, and that you aren't going to suddenly change your mind after they've invested days or weeks of effort. *Especially* if it's because you either haven't thought it through, or you are bowing to political pressure to save yourself at the expense of the team.

Your creative team wants to trust you. In fact, it *needs* to trust you in order to do its work. If, however, the team has to screech to a halt just before a "right turn" because your direction has changed at the last minute or because things aren't quite the way you promised they would be, your words will cease to mean much. Instead, it will creep along at a cautious pace until the team members see the turn with their own eyes.

Most smart, conscientious leaders don't blow trust in the big areas. They don't overtly lie to their team or intentionally neglect it. No, most leaders of creative teams forfeit trust in little ways that they don't even consider until it's too late. That's what we'll focus on in this chapter, because these seemingly insignificant areas of compromised trust are ignored by many leaders, and they don't see the effects until it's too late.

When your team trusts you, people believe in what you say, *and* they believe that you do too. You are not trying to manipulate them into doing something that's against their best interest. Rather, team members know that you are willing to take an arrow if necessary for them because you care more about the team's interests and outcomes than your personal ones. This is incredibly important for creative work, because the team needs to be able to trust that you will protect it from the onslaught of demands and will strive to help it find the space people need to do work they can be proud of. If your team doesn't trust you, people won't work comfortably within the creative rails that you've set, because they will always be in fear that things will change. No one wants to waste effort knowing the creative direction is inclined to shift with the political winds.

TRUST IS NOT STATIC

Pat was a relative newcomer at an agency where he became known for his willingness to speak truth to the people in charge. In fact, it was his willingness to say and do what was necessary that led to his quick promotion through the ranks. "Everyone trusted me, especially my teammates, because they knew that I would always speak the truth, even when it wasn't popular," he told me. He was known as a champion for the team, one of the voices that would always speak up when something didn't seem right. However, once he was promoted over some of his peers, things got complicated. Instead of seeing him as a champion for the team, his former peers saw him as a part of the establishment. It was much more difficult for him to earn the trust of the people who once cheered him on, because they recognized that he now had authority over them and had certain information that they weren't privy to. Every action he took was suddenly a referendum on his trustworthiness. He felt like they were constantly waiting for any misstep.

Trust is not stored up like money in a bank account, where if you spend some a little bit foolishly, you still have some left in the account. It's more like a water balloon. You can fill up the balloon over time, but if you puncture it once, even with a tiny hole, you lose all of the water. Similarly, you typically don't lose trust in only one area. If you prove yourself to be untrustworthy in one situation, people tend to generalize that lack of trustworthiness to other areas as well. A small and careless lie about an upcoming meeting suddenly morphs into a complete meltdown of trust on a huge client project.

You earn trust when the things you *say* line up with the things you *do*. It's that simple. However, this is not as easy as it sounds, because as a leader you face many pressures that are invisible to the people on your team. You might feel a need to make promises in the heat of the moment ("If you work on Saturday, I'll give you next Friday off") that you might not be able to keep. You might say something to ease an emotionally difficult moment ("Next time, I will give you ownership of that project") that you come to regret later. You might say something to ease your own insecurity ("You're right—he *is* wronging you") that conflicts with one of your team's core principles. All of these things would result in a breach of trust. Even little things, like starting and ending meetings on time, honoring and not canceling scheduled one-on-one chats, and always abiding by rules you set for the team, make a big impact on trust. Although any of these in isolation might not seem like a big deal, they become a real problem the next time you need someone on you team to take a risk on your behalf or trust a promise that you've made.

There are three small, overlooked "don'ts" and three often forgotten "dos" that help you earn and maintain the trust of the creative people on your team.

DON'T DECLARE UNDECLARABLES

A few years ago, a bear was spotted in southwest Ohio, a few counties away from where my family and I live. Because bears aren't native to our area, the local news was plastered with sightings and updates on the bear's activity, even though it was probably sixty or more miles outside of the metropolitan area. I could tell that our kids were a little nervous about the prospects of running into the bear while playing soccer in the backyard or on a walk around the neighborhood, so I reassured them that there was no chance—none at all—that we'd ever see the bear. After all, the area where it was spotted was at least an hour's drive by car, and it was in a rural area, which was its natural habitat. There was zero chance that it would ever come anywhere close to the city. It was a happy bear. The kids seemed relieved, and we kind of forgot about it all. For a while.

About a week later, as I was driving to the gym, I spotted a news crew camped out at the bottom of our street. Apparently, the bear had been spotted that morning in the woods a block from our house. Two runners saw it dart across the road and down into the creek, where our kids regularly play. In fact, I'd walked through those woods the night before. Over the

You typically don't lose trust in only one area. If you prove yourself to be untrustworthy in one situation, people tend to generalize that lack of trustworthiness to other areas as well.

coming week, we heard many stories from neighbors about how the bear had been in their garbage cans, or how they'd seen it run across their backyard at twilight. No one knows what eventually became of the bear. We assume that it eventually found its way southward into Kentucky and beyond, but for those few days it seemed to pop up in several of the places our family tends to frequent.

Let's just say that Dad lost a little bit of credibility because of the "bear incident." For a while afterward, whenever I'd make a declarative statement about something, the kids would tease me: "Now, is this *really* true, or is this like the bear thing?" It took me awhile to gain back their trust.

The lesson? No matter how unlikely the chances of something occurring are, avoid making a declarative statement that could eventually prove false. Yes, the odds are that we'd never see the bear in a million years, but my kids don't care about the odds. They only care about not getting mauled while chasing the ice cream truck. And now, the one person they trust to protect them has proved that he isn't a trustworthy source of information. Not good.

It's tempting to make declarative statements in the face of uncertainty, especially when you know the odds are good for your prediction's coming true. This is especially tempting in creative work, where there is so much uncertainty that a little bit of solid ground makes everyone feel better for a while and relieves the pressure on you as a leader. It positions you as the authority. It stops the incessant questioning. It even makes you seem more confident and may appear to build trust for a while. For instance, it was easier and more convenient for me to say there was no chance of seeing the bear than to say, "Well, it could happen, but probably won't," because my objective was to relieve my kids' fear. However, it only takes one of those declarative statements to be wrong to lose trust in every area.

Are you taking declarative positions that you *probably* shouldn't (such as, "The client's going to love this—you're done," or "We are definitely going with your idea this time")? Is your team absolutely counting on something that might not happen, or are people latching on to your promise that something won't happen that very well could? If so, any of these situations is a possible breach of trust just waiting to happen. And that means that they won't be able to trust you when the pressure is on and what you say *really* matters.

When facing difficult odds, it's (almost) always better to be realistic with the team than to offer up declarative statements. If you've hired smart, mature people, then let them deal with the uncertainty—treat them like adults. (However, you don't have to dump everything on them at once. As a leader, you will always know things that they don't, and they only need to deal with what's relevant to their work at any given time.) Remember, trust is hard earned but easily lost.

Also, don't allow your own assumptions to cause you to mislead your team. For example, my assumption that the bear would never come close to the city was factually incorrect, even though it sounded great (and reassuring) at the time to my kids. Make sure that you have your facts straight before making a declarative statement to the team. Don't wait until you see a bear digging through your trashcan to realize that you were wrong.

DON'T BE A SUPERHERO

As the leader, it's natural to want your team to think you have all the answers. It's tempting to think that they will trust you more if you are always the smartest person

Question: Is there any situation in which you have made a declarative statement to relieve your team's concerns but that could breach your trust in the long run?

in the room. That's why it's challenging for many leaders to invite other people into their thought process. Instead, they feel the need to act like a superhero, invulnerable to attack and able to leap tall problems with a single bound. However, no amount of posturing can cover up the truth. No matter how invulnerable you pretend to be, everyone can see the truth, and often the harder you to try to cover it up, the more apparent it becomes. That's a great way to lose the trust of your team, because people can tell that you are simply pretending to have it all together. It's better to let your guard down and allow others into your thought process. This not only earns trust, but it broadens your perspective on the problem. That's a win-win.

Bill Taylor, founder of *Fast Company* magazine, told me that effective leaders hold two attributes in tension: ambition and humility. "Leaders have to believe deeply in themselves and what they're doing. People want to be led by those who exude personal strength." That's the superhero part of the equation. Having confidence is different, however, from pretending you are always the smartest person in the room. He says that you have to be willing to listen to others and admit that you don't always have all of the answers. This is not just good for the team; it's good for business because it keeps you from projecting to the team that your ideas are the only ones that matter.

Avoiding superhero syndrome is accomplished in two ways: being authentic and being (appropriately) vulnerable. If you want people to follow you, make building an authentic relationship with them a primary concern. You can fake relational connection for a while, but trust will fall apart under stress. You lose their trust.

Being (appropriately) vulnerable means allowing people on your team to see that you recognize your own strengths and weaknesses and that you value self-awareness. Rather than trying to pretend that you have all the answers, be vulnerable enough to invite team members into the decision-making process in order to help you (and them) gain better perspective. Great leaders are open about the factors they are weighing ("On one hand, this idea helps us with X. However, the other option addresses Y. Which do you think is most important?"). They also know when to have frank conversations about the potential consequences of their decisions ("Here's what I'm concerned about with this new direction. What do *you* think?"). Being open about all possible outcomes shows team members that you're really in the trenches with them.

Now, appropriate vulnerability means that you don't want to dump everything you're thinking on your team. There are some things that are simply not for public consumption. Let's face it: we've all known leaders who lack this simple discernment. (Mentally insert your favorite Michael Scott scene from *The Office* here.) *Appropriate* vulnerability means inviting your team into your thoughts, not treating it like a therapist.

Here are a few things to consider:

Is there a decision you're currently trying to make that you could invite others into as a way of modeling your thought process and building trust?

Does your team have to guess at what influences your decisions, or are you regularly communicating your principles and inviting input?

Is there any way in which you might be selling out your team at the moment, whether that means shifting blame or protecting yourself? If so, you're playing a dangerous game with the team's trust and, frankly, with your career as well.

By letting down your guard, you not only appear more human to your team (imagine that!), you also earn its trust. Here are a few tactics for countering the temptation to play the superhero.

Tell a story about a time you made a poor decision and what you learned from it. By showing that you recognize your mistakes, your team will see that you aren't wearing blinders. Take some time to think of a handful of stories and lessons that you can pull out at an appropriate moment, and always have them at the ready. However, be selective in how you use these stories so that they don't become predictable or elicit snark and cynicism ("Oh great—here comes the 'I haven't always been the perfect specimen you see before you' lecture"). You're not preaching at people; you're showing others that you've made recoverable mistakes and that sometimes mistakes can be the foundation for progress. (More about telling stories in a few pages.)

If necessary, offer up the first dumb idea. Sometimes people are afraid to share ideas because they don't want to look bad in front of the group. If you share something that's obviously subpar, others will think. *Well, at least my idea isn't that bad!* When the person in charge is willing to say something that's obviously not that good, it gives others permission to speak freely. Often, their ideas are better than they fear. By demonstrating that the world doesn't end with a bad idea, you're establishing the safety of the environment and of you as a leader.

> By showing that you recognize your mistakes, your team will see that you aren't wearing blinders.

Admit when you're intimidated. People on your creative team are much better than you at many things. Let them know that you respect their ability. In fact, when someone else is better than you at something, don't be afraid to tell them that you're a little intimidated. By honestly sharing where you feel overmatched, you'll show them that you recognize that there are areas where you still need to grow. Don't fall back into complete deference to the other person—that's just awkward—but confidently acknowledge that you'd love for them to help you better understand what they're doing. It's a great way to build common ground and to show that you respect them. Your candidness will likely earn their trust in return.

Act as if trust must be won through every conversation, action, and decision. If you do, then you'll never struggle to have the goodwill you need to lead your team in uncertain times.

It's also important to note an additional factor in avoiding the superhero temptation: warmth. In their book *Friend and Foe*, about the nature of competition and cooperation, researchers Adam Galinsky and Maurice Schweitzer detail its importance: "Competence alone is insufficient. Whether it's on the campaign trail or negotiating a high-stakes deal, we also need warmth." They argue that a key element of trust is a willingness to show a side of yourself that you might be tempted to protect if you were trying to be a superhero. That can mean telling a self-deprecating joke, making an honest confession, or delivering a terribly off-key karaoke performance at the office party. All of this reveals your human side and forges bonding. They go on to say that "[t]he effectiveness of this strategy debunks the common assumption that trust is something that can only be built *slowly* over time." Don't do something that is out of character for you, because that will seem just as inauthentic as being perfectly stoic all the time. (As a card-carrying introvert, I can fully understand the desire to grab a drink and hide behind a plant in the corner at any gathering of more than three people.) The important principle here is to look for opportunities to show your true colors to the team and let people see that there is a person behind the job title.

However, Galinsky and Schweitzer also caution that you must be careful when expressing vulnerability, because it can backfire if you fail to establish credibility first. Vulnerability alone does not inspire trust unless the person is first seen to be skilled and capable. In other words, don't walk into the team meeting on the first day and spill your coffee, expecting relational nirvana.

DON'T ENGAGE IN RELATIONAL USURY

In the classic book *Tom Sawyer*, Tom is punished for skipping school by being forced to whitewash a fence. As he's reluctantly painting, he sees his friend Ben Rogers walking by. Ben laughs at Tom's punishment, but Tom insightfully tells Ben that it's no punishment at all; he's actually enjoying himself. Ben begs to have a chance to work on the fence, and Tom hands over the brush, pretending to be put out. More friends come by, and one by one Tom works out a deal with each for a turn on the fence. Not only did Tom get out of painting, but he actually wound up with a pocket full of toys.

The story paints Tom as a shrewd businessman, negotiating his way out of the hard work while reaping all the benefits. In the short run, this kind of strategy probably worked well for him, but it's likely that his friends soon caught on to his tricks. It's just like a client who realizes that they have been overpaying for the same service their competitor is getting much cheaper, or the designer who learns that working extra hours and weekends on that project didn't really improve her standing within the company. The person with power ends up with all of the benefits, but all that's left in the end is a lack of trust.

Think about it: if you suspect that someone only sees you as a means to an end, you are probably (rightfully) skeptical when they offer to do you a favor. You're always looking for the angle, even if it seems like they are serving you. It's not necessarily that they have said anything in this instance to warrant your skepticism; it's that their entire body of interaction with you triggers alarm bells anytime there is an exchange of value. As a leader, you obviously can't afford this kind of baseline distrust.

Still, it's tempting in the moment to overplay the potential benefits of a project or to promise some future benefit for a little bit of sacrifice now. ("If you work this Saturday, I'll give you next Friday off. Oh—sorry. Something came up and we need you to work Friday after all.") This kind of behavior amounts to what I call relational usury. "Usury" means the lending of money at ridiculously high rates of interest. The lender is taking advantage of the borrower, because they know that the situation is desperate and they'll take any offer. (Or, in some cases, the borrower is ignorant of the consequences of his actions.) Relational usury means that you are leveraging your relative power over the other person to get them to agree to something that really isn't in her own best interest.

Relational usury isn't always intentional. You might genuinely believe—in the moment—that you can deliver on your word. However, you should never promise anything—a raise, an assignment, a recommendation—you don't have every intention of moving heaven and earth to fulfill. If you do, you are essentially manipulating people in order to get what you want now, even if it means that you are sacrificing their trust later.

Don't borrow against future trust in order to reap an immediate return. Unless the fate of the free world is at stake, it is foolish to compromise your team's willingness to trust you tomorrow in order

Question: Are there ways in which you are engaging in relational usury with members of your team? To accomplish something in the short term, are you making promises of a future benefit that you might not be able to keep?

to achieve a goal today. Effective leaders pause to consider the long-term consequences of their actions.

DO PROTECT YOUR TEAM'S RESOURCES

In the world of creative work, execution is king. A brilliant idea is worthless if you aren't able to make it happen. Most of your team's ideas will be executed in the form of projects, and leading the charge means establishing the strategy, ensuring that there are clear expectations, and making certain that your team has the resources it needs in order to do its best work.

However, perhaps the most important role you play is to be decisive at the exact moment your team needs you to be. Your team needs you to be very clear about what you expect from it and when, and the team members need you to achieve buy-in from critical stakeholders so that there is no danger of "scope creep" (expectations rise in the midst of a project), or buyer's remorse (the stakeholders begin to second-guess their decisions and ask to change the direction of the project after the work has already begun). A lack of clear buy-in from stakeholders at critical moments is a common cause of frustration and burnout for creative teams, and it's a key reason why leaders lose trust. When expectations change on a whim throughout the project, the team eventually learns to just wait and see what happens before applying any real effort.

Doug, a senior leader of a creative team, dreaded midproject conversations with his manager, especially after the weekend. The manager always seemed to come in on Monday with an epiphany about a project already in process. Every time they met he would layer another request on the team. He'd say, "Hey, could we just do X, or please have the team check into Y?" Individually, most were small requests, so he didn't see the harm. The team, however, felt the weight of the aggregate requests over time, and Doug was not very good at setting boundaries. The constantly changing scope often meant that the team was scrambling to meet the manager's requests right up until the project was due, which meant that establishing a predictable pace of work was nearly impossible. The team always felt like it was behind.

As you navigate your team through a project, it's your job to set expectations both with your team and with your own managers and stakeholders. If you fail to do so, your team will pay the price and you will lose their trust.

Make a decision once, then move on. Some team members like to revisit every choice that is made, especially if they disagree with the original decision. They continually share why their idea is better, or why the current strategy is destined to fail, even after everyone has already begun work on it. You can't allow these conversations to happen, or they will undermine your team's confidence. Your job is to make tough calls, and constantly revisiting every single decision will waste focus and energy that should be spent delivering results.

By the way, this doesn't apply only to the people who report to you. Beg your own leader(s) not to call decisions into question in front of your team once the work has begun. If they want to have those conversations in private, so be it; but if your team feels like the strategy is being questioned, it could cause them to lose trust in you.

Clearly communicate the consequences of decisions to the stake-holders. Those making decisions should understand that resources and time will be allocated against those decisions, and that changing direction later—especially once you're in midproject—will be extremely costly. It's as if a giant three-foot-wide steel door has closed behind you as you make a decision, and it's closed you off. Of course, it's possible to go back through the door, but it's going to require a tremendous amount of effort and it's going to be costly to do so. Help your own leader understand that changing his mind later will mean that other work will be neglected or organizational resources will be wasted correcting a decision that wasn't fully thought through from the beginning. Also, *never* surprise people who have the ability to override your decisions. Don't put your leader or your team in a situation where a simple lack of awareness of what you're doing leads to wasted effort and resources.

Reinforce your decisions with frequent touch points. It's often the case that stakeholders lose touch with a project after a key decision is made and work begins. Don't allow them to become so disconnected from the work that they lose touch with the reasoning behind the original decisions, some of which might have been made weeks or months ago. It's not uncommon for people to get cold feet, especially if the direction was a little risky. Remind them of why the decision was made and why it's *still* the right one.

DO TELL A GOOD STORY

Lisa Johnson has spent years studying the elements of effective storytelling and has become a sought-after consultant by some of the world's largest brands. She believes that one of the best ways for leaders to show themselves to their team is through telling stories.

Specifically, she says that leaders should tell stories that reveal something about themselves that the team may not have previously heard.

Don't borrow against future trust in order to reap an immediate return.

Following are a few kinds of stories that Johnson recommends leaders tell.

Family and foundation stories. One way to earn your team's trust is to show people where you "come from." Help team members see that your viewpoints are not just a matter of recent convenience, but that they've been forged over a lifetime of experience. Family and foundation stories reveal something about how your character and worldview were formed. "This is when the leader tells a personal story of when they learned something from a mentor, or a family member, that has stuck with them to this day," Johnson explained. The stories provide a sense of grounding and help people gain context for how you see the world and make decisions. They also show that you are teachable and willing to learn things from important people in your life. Make sure that the story has a clear and discernible point. The goal isn't just to tell stories; it's to provide context and connection for your team.

Here are a few questions to help you identify some family and foundation stories:

Is there a teacher or a mentor who has taught you something valuable that still serves you to this day?

Was there anything quirky about your family that shaped the way you work or see the world?

Was there a time when someone said something to you that changed your trajectory?

Motivations and milestones. Was there a time when you worked hard and accomplished something that meant a lot to you? Telling these stories can help your team see what drives you and help people connect with the most meaningful moments in your life. It's important for the team to see you accomplishing things in your personal life outside of the journey you are taking together.

Was there a big goal that you set and accomplished? How did it feel, and what did you learn?

Was there a time when you did the right thing, even though it was difficult?

Was there a moment in your life when you took a calculated risk and it paid off? What happened?

Mistakes and learnings. Finally, share stories of times when you made mistakes and learned from them. It's important for your team to see that you recognize your own shortcomings as opportunities to grow. It helps people believe you when you tell them to take their own risks and push the edges creatively. "Behavior is more caught than taught," Johnson told me. If you expect your team to take risks, you have to show that you walk your talk.

Was there a time when you failed in a very public way? What happened, and what did you learn from it?

What is the most embarrassing thing that has happened to you professionally, and how did you recover?

Have you ever had to apologize to someone for something you said or did? What happened, and what did you learn?

Make a practice of collecting stories for later use whenever they come to mind. You might even want to keep them in a notebook or a place where you can find them easily. The important thing is that they should have a clear point, and they should inspire your team to deeper levels of trust. "Always have a point to your story. Show growth. Show how you've learned and evolved, don't just tell stories to try to connect," Johnson said.

She also advised that an effective way of identifying stories is to use a "fill in the blank" method. For example:

"I had a personal breakthrough when

_____."

Exercise: Take thirty minutes this week to identify some stories from your life that you can share with your team.

"I'll never forget the day _____."

"I'll never forget when I met _____."

"If I had the guts, I would _____."

With some time and thought, you'll soon have a treasure trove of stories you can use to inspire your team.

DO CHANGE YOUR MIND (SOMETIMES)

You know that vision is important for a leader. If you don't know where you're headed, you'll certainly never inspire someone to follow you there.

However, for leaders of creative people it's not fixed vision that defines whether you're trustworthy, it's *adaptive* vision. An effective leader is able to spot shifting patterns in the environment and shift strategy in order to take advantage of them, all the while moving the team toward the end goal.

To some people, changing your mind—especially in a highly public way—has become sin number one. If a politician or business leader evolves in his understanding of a topic, we call him a flip-flopper. If someone alters her once fierce perspective in light of new-found information, we call her a hypocrite or a traitor.

However, one of the most crucial roles of the leader is to be a learner, and it is impossible to learn without your thoughts being shaped and changed in some way. Trustworthy leaders are open to the idea that they don't know everything and that their present understanding could be wrong, or at least incomplete.

I would even go so far as to say that if you've not changed your mind about something in the past few years, you may be less than intellectually honest or lacking in curiosity. Fossilizing around your hypotheses is a lazy way to approach life and work, and in the end it will result in a compromised body of work.

> **If you've not changed your mind about something in the past few years, you may be less than intellectually honest or lacking in curiosity.**

Are you allowing your ideas to evolve over time? Are you willing to adapt if your thoughts are proved to be incomplete or inadequate? Or do you feel a need to defend your ideas regardless of contrary information?

An important caveat: changing your mind doesn't mean being intellectually lazy until you *have* to take a side. That's just procrastination. I'm talking about true, well-thought-out opinions that simply change because of new information. And you will have to take your team on the journey with you as you change your mind. One leader described it to me as like traveling along a chain of islands. You might be on the last island in the chain, and your team is on the first. You can't expect it to skip all of the islands to get to where you are in one step. You have to go back to the first island and help the team make the same journey you made, from island to island, in changing your mind. Talking people through your process helps them see not only what you're thinking, but why you're thinking it. That will earn you great trust and will reinforce the team's overall vision and passion for the new direction.

Legendary leadership expert Warren Bennis said, "Trust is the lubrication that makes it possible for organizations to work." Strive daily to earn the trust of your team. You will have moments of failure, of course, but as the people on your team see that you truly have their best interest at heart, and as they see your personal motivations more clearly, your effectiveness will grow, and you'll begin to see your influence scale in ways you didn't expect.

CHECKPOINT

Managing trust on your team is an ongoing effort. Strive to align your words with your actions.

Actions

—Identify any "undeclarables" that you've shared with the team and that could be a ticking "trust time bomb." How do you need to clarify with your team?

—Offer up the first dumb idea in a meeting this week.

—Tell a story about an important mentor or coach in your life and what you learned.

Conversations

Have a conversation with key team members about the following:

—Is there any place where you think my stated expectations are out of alignment with my actual expectations?

—Invite a key team member into a decision you're making, show her your thought process, and ask her advice.

Rituals

These rituals are also collected at the end of the book under weekly, monthly, and quarterly categories so that you can engage in them regularly.

Weekly: Reflect on current projects and where you may be allowing expectation escalation to overwhelm the rhythm of your team. Are you setting bait-and-switch expectations with your team?

Monthly: Consider the past month of work. Have there been any breaches of trust on your part? Do you need to make it right with someone?

Quarterly: Identify a few stories from your past that you might want to share with the team at an opportune time. These can be times when you failed and learned something, a story from your childhood, or anything else that humanizes you to the team.

CHAPTER 7

PRUNE PROACTIVELY

Shaping Your Culture

A culture is like an immune system. It operates through the laws of systems, just like a body. If a body has an infection, the immune system deals with it. Similarly, a group enforces its norms, either actively or passively.

—Dr. Henry Cloud

PRINCIPLE: To create stability, you have to actively grow a healthy culture.

Have you ever walked into a company's headquarters and passed an enormous marble wall engraved with the company's values? There it is, in all its permanence and glory, greeting employees each day and reminding them: "THIS IS WHO WE ARE!"

Except, it's not always. It's who they *were*, once. Most people walk right past that wall without even paying it a moment of notice. They're numb to it, and it doesn't really hold any sway over their everyday behavior. Your culture isn't defined by a set of tenets or a plaque on the wall. It's defined by what you *do*.

If you say that you value boldness but always make the most comfortable decision, then people will cease to be bold.

If you say that you value customer service, but you are always snickering and telling stories about how annoying your customers are, then you will train your culture to devalue its customers.

If you say that you value truth telling, but you get defensive every time someone attempts to offer a piece of constructive feedback, you will cultivate a reactive, closed-minded culture.

This kind of hypocrisy is demoralizing. However, with clear ground rules and a stable culture around your team, creative people know they have the support they need to take risks. Your team's experience of you *is* its experience of the company. Period. Full stop. When cultural expectations aren't well defined, people tend to be very conservative out of a fear of getting it wrong.

Dee Hock, founder and former CEO of Visa, once said, "Simple, clear purpose and principles give rise to complex and intelligent behavior. Complex rules and regulations give rise to simple and stupid behavior." However, you cannot impose a culture on a team. Great cultures are grown from the ground up. A culture mandated from on high will fit like a suit that's three sizes too large, never quite cut to size.

With clear ground rules and a stable culture around your team, creative people know they have the support they need to take risks.

Because cultures are grown, you must treat yours like a garden. Just like a good gardener, you aggressively fertilize the aspects of your team's culture that you want in abundance and diligently prune the things you want to get rid of. This requires constant attention on your part, because if you allow a few errant behaviors to slide, you will eventually find your entire garden choked with weeds.

How do you know which aspects of the culture to prune and which to fertilize? As we discussed in chapter 3, you must first define your core leadership principles, then codify them so that they are easily understood and adopted by the team. However, that alone isn't sufficient. Be on the lookout for any areas of misalignment with those core cultural principles and prune them before they have the chance to take root. Then fertilize the good behavior you want to see more of.

PRUNE THE "GHOST RULES"

Ella was a successful manager at a very large company. I was challenging her to think in a new way about a tricky problem she was attempting to solve, but when I offered my thought, she quickly responded, "Nope—that won't work here."

I paused, a little stunned at her abruptness, and asked, "Why not?"

She looked at me as if collecting her thoughts, and after a few moments she replied, "Hmm. Good question." After further dissection, we realized that Ella's response had been hardwired into her by a previous manager, who often had strong, fear-based opinions about new ideas. "That won't work here" was a common reaction to many of Ella's fresh thoughts, and over time she began to adopt these opinions as hard fact.

What Ella had come up against are what I call ghost rules, or invisible limitations that people or teams place upon themselves for no good reason. Sometimes these rules become baked-in organizational assumptions about what is and isn't possible, and the net result is that the team artificially limits the places it looks for ideas or value.

In order for your team to feel freedom to do its best work,

regularly prune ghost rules from your life and your team's culture. Following are a few examples of ghost rules I frequently see.

What Will and Won't Work?

A manager from a large company once told me that he was instructed not to pursue a particular idea because "someone tried that back in the 1980s, and it didn't work." Apart from the laws of physics, a lot of things have changed in the past thirty years. It's probably wise to revisit some of these baked-in organizational assumptions from time to time, just like Ella did, and ensure that you're not missing potentially valuable insights.

Is your team paralyzed because of assumptions or narratives about what will and won't work? Challenge any declarative statement by asking "Why?" If you do not receive an answer, then it's possible that the team is operating by assumption, not fact.

Who Can and Can't Introduce an Idea?

Some teams have invisible rules about who is allowed to contribute ideas to a project or who is allowed to offer thoughts or criticism about a decision. Although you do need to have a protocol for sharing ideas and offering critiques, narrowing your scope of vision to just a handful of people can be extremely limiting. Ensure that everyone on the team understands clearly what's expected of them and the *actual* process for sharing feedback or ideas, not the perceived one.

Are team members limiting their feedback or shrinking back from offering insights because they feel it's not their place to do so?

Identify and eliminate these ghost rules from your culture by replacing them—in the moment you catch them—with the principles that you want reinforce. In meetings, call on people who never share and ask them to offer their opinions. Invite new people to meetings who are always on the outside. Shake up the assumptions with actions that are rooted instead in your core principles.

What Is and Isn't Acceptable Behavior?

Expectation escalation can quickly take over a team's culture and turn it into a pressure cooker. When a team member decides to come in at 7 a.m. one morning, another makes it 6:45 a.m. the following morning. Then 6:30 a.m. Pretty soon, the cultural thermostat is set, and the assumed behavior is "we are a culture that expects people to arrive to work before the sun rises." No one ever stated it explicitly, but all new hires observed the behavior and they assume "this must be the way it is around here." That's just one example of how certain behaviors can become assumptive expectations without ever having been explicitly stated.

Are there behaviors on your team that are assumed to be expectations but are in fact simply a result of expectation escalation? Identify and squelch them.

The worst part about ghost rules is that some leaders actually use them to manipulate the team into achieving the results they want, regardless of the negative consequences. They might allow team members to believe certain things to be true—working weekends is expected, e-mail responses within minutes are required, challenging certain people's ideas is off-limits—in order to make their own life easier. This kind of manipulation works for a while, but it will catch up with them over time. Although people might comply with the ghost rules in order to keep their jobs, these leaders will not maintain the trust and respect of their team for long.

You want your creative team operating by simple, clear principles so that it can be messy and risky with the work it does. If people are wasting their mental energy just trying to comply with invisible barriers that no one has really set for them, they will feel disempowered and unable to bring their full heart and soul to the work.

Once you've collected all of the ghost rules that you believe no longer have a place in your organization, have a conversation with your team about them. When you do, pair them with the counterprinciple that you'd like your team to live by.

Exercise: Identify any ghost rules that your team is following. These could be residual rules from a previous leader or organizational rules that you need to prune. Replace them with a counterprinciple.

For example, if you're canceling an assumed, recurring meeting (which is redundant and useless, but it has happened every week since 1971 because, well, bagels), reinforce a principle that states something like: "We value one another's time and only call meetings to achieve an important, defined outcome." Or if you want to increase collaboration, replace a rule about who can and cannot introduce ideas with: "The best ideas can come from anywhere, so we are all free to share what's on our mind." It's important not just to eliminate old habits, but to fill the void with the new principle.

CHESTERTON'S FENCE AND CHEKHOV'S GUN

When you are pruning existing elements of the culture, be careful not to act solely on your first instincts. There may be elements of the culture that are in place for reasons you don't know.

Anton Chekhov, the famed Russian playwright, is reported to have given this advice to his fellow writers: "Remove everything that has no relevance to the story. If you say in the first chapter that there is a rifle hanging on the wall, in the second or third chapter it absolutely must go off. If it's not going to be fired, it shouldn't be hanging there." In the context of a play, this means that every detail that's included in the writing—such as a loaded rifle on the wall—should be relevant to the plot and should in some way advance the story. If not, it should be removed because it is nothing but a distraction.

Often, we leave legacy goals or processes in place even though they are irrelevant to the very mission that we're trying to instill in our team. These systems are like a loaded rifle left hanging on the wall: everyone wonders whether and when it's going to be used, and it distracts from the core story line.

However, there is a counterpoint to this argument. In his book *The Thing*, theologian G. K. Chesterton offered words of wisdom that I believe apply to any leader bent on creating change inside an organization. "There exists in such a case a certain institution or law; let us say, for the sake of simplicity, a fence or gate erected across a road. The more modern type of reformer goes gaily up to it and says, 'I don't see the use of this; let us clear it away.' To which the more intelligent type of reformer will do well to answer: 'If you don't see the use of it, I certainly won't let you clear it away. Go away and think. Then, when you can come back and tell me that you do see the use of it, I may allow you to destroy it.'"

So don't allow seemingly pointless legacy meetings on your team calendar, but don't cut them until you understand their real purpose.

In his rashness, a leader may prune something that serves a perfectly good, though not immediately apparent, purpose. In fact, to Chesterton's point, the very fact that you don't understand why something exists is a good reason to pause before you prune.

PRUNE ANY "NORMALIZATION OF DEVIANCE"

In 2003, what was supposed to be a routine space shuttle mission ended in disaster as *Columbia* unexpectedly broke apart during reentry to the Earth's atmosphere. After an intensive investigation, NASA discovered that the cause of the disaster was an anomaly during the launch of the *Columbia* a few weeks earlier. A piece of foam had broken off from the external tank used to propel the shuttle into orbit, and it struck the wing of the spacecraft, doing unknowable amounts of damage. Given the fact that the damage was unlikely to be repairable by the *Columbia* crew, ground control opted not to inform them, and the mission proceeded as expected, until the disastrous reentry. The investigation revealed that the damage caused by the dislodged foam to the wing of the shuttle was so extensive that it caused the shuttle to become unstable and break apart upon hitting the Earth's atmosphere, killing all of the crew members instantly.

What made the *Columbia* disaster even more disturbing was that the phenomenon that caused it—the breaking off of foam from the external tank—was not a one-time event. In fact, foam had broken off from the tank on several previous missions, and those missions had completed successfully. (Due to the common nature of the malfunction, NASA even coined the phrase "foam shedding" to describe it.) Because there were no immediate consequences resulting from the malfunction on prior missions, it was essentially considered "safe" by Mission Control, and was widely accepted as a possible anomaly during a launch.

This wasn't the first disaster of this nature to befall NASA. In fact, sociologist Diane Vaughn had conducted research on a previous space shuttle disaster—the *Challenger* explosion in 1986—and determined that the ultimate cause of the disaster was the widespread acceptance of minor deviations from safety protocol over time that eventually became culturally accepted. She wrote, "Social normalization of deviance means that people within the organization become so much accustomed to a deviant behavior that they don't consider it as deviant, despite the fact that they far exceed their own rules for the elementary safety." Minor compromises over time by a handful of individuals become widely accepted compromises by the culture at large. Although seemingly innocent at first, these minor compromises can eventually yield unforeseen major and even catastrophic consequences. She continued, "As [NASA] recurrently observed the problem with no consequence they got to the point that flying with the flaw was normal and acceptable."

This kind of "normalization of deviance" shows up in nearly every organization. Over time, small and seemingly insignificant compromises are made that begin to erode the precision and clarity of the team and eventually begin to degrade the culture. You cannot be successful and disciplined in the big things if you are undisciplined about the small ones. Your inattention to detail will eventually catch up with you.

As a leader, when you signal tacit acceptance of deviant behavior, you are playing a dangerous game. Small, public compromises can erode the team's trust, or that of your client, and essentially give permission for everyone else to follow suit. Here are a few places where you should look for behavior that could seem innocent in the moment but could wind up being disastrous in the long run.

Minor Missed Deadlines

"Oh, no problem. Just get it to me tomorrow." Sometimes this is an acceptable response to late work if there are unexpected factors involved, but be sure that you're not creating a culture in which all deadlines have air quotes around them because no one really takes them seriously. If you overlook minor missed deadlines, it makes it harder to impose urgency later, over more important ones.

Skipped Meetings

I was once caught off guard by a comment someone on my team made. "Oh, if you have a meeting scheduled with Todd, chances are about fifty percent it'll actually happen." I thought that I was actually giving the team member more freedom by routinely canceling meetings that didn't need to happen, but it turns out that I was only thinking about things from my own perspective. For the team member, time with me provided a chance to influence decisions and connect. Although I was thinking only pragmatically, there was much more at stake. Worse, I was creating an environment in which canceling meetings at the last minute was acceptable behavior, which made it difficult to plan the week effectively.

As a leader, when you signal tacit acceptance of deviant behavior, you are playing a dangerous game.

Keep your commitments; however, when

you have to cancel one, make certain that both parties agree that it's the right decision.

Disrespectful Tone

Tolerance of snarky tones or biting sarcasm in meetings can degrade an otherwise healthy or emotionally safe culture. That's not to say that there isn't room for playfulness and edge, but make sure the tone is respectful and doesn't take a dark turn. Again, culture rises and falls based upon what is tolerated. Create an environment in which everyone feels safe to express their opinions while also ensuring that those opinions are expressed with respect for the other people present. It sounds obvious and easy, but it's not, especially when hurt feelings are involved.

Talking Behind Someone's Back

This one is simple: if you have something to say about someone, say it to the person's face. If you allow others to talk to you about a co-worker in a way that's disrespectful or that dehumanizes the person, then you are creating a culture in which everyone eventually becomes paranoid. Never talk about someone in a way that you wouldn't if that person was in the room with you; otherwise, you will model and tacitly endorse this behavior throughout the team.

Acceptable Shortcuts or Subpar Work (Without Reason)

The enemy of brilliant is "good enough." When you choose to cut corners in a public way, you are telling the team that it's OK to do the same, and over time everyone will succumb to mediocrity. There are definitely times when you need to compromise on quality due to constraints such as time or budget, but ensure that these compromises are explained and that everyone knows why they were necessary in that specific instance.

Now, some of this might seem very minor. After all, we've all been a part of teams that exhibit these behaviors and yet held together just fine. Some of those teams might have been highly productive. However, don't confuse delayed consequences with no consequences. Although you may not reap the negative effects of small compromises now, you eventually will. Dysfunctional cultures often begin with a series of seemingly insignificant choices to normalize mediocrity, and those minor choices have major ramifications down the road. Great leadership isn't about what you can get away with now; it's about growing a culture in which your team can thrive for a long time to come.

When you notice acts of deviance beginning to pop up, have a conversation with the individual. Don't call the person out in front of the team unless the act is so egregious that it demands a public response. With empathy, help the person understand why the behavior is not acceptable and encourage with the counterprinciple that you're trying to instill in the team.

Question: Are there areas where you are tolerating small acts of deviant behavior and are in danger of normalizing it?

"FERTILIZE" BY REWARDING WHAT YOU WANT TO SEE AT SCALE

On the other hand, consider what you are rewarding and what that says about what you *truly* value. If you routinely issue one set of expectations but reward something different (even unknowingly), then you are likely to get undesired results. Ensure that your rewards align with your expectations. By rewards, I don't just mean financial rewards, but also words of affirmation in front of the team, offers of work that is more personally gratifying or allows more autonomy, or even a new position.

As an example, many leaders talk about how they value strategic risk and encourage their employees to push limits and explore new ideas, but then they quickly reward more expected ideas and shun those that could pose risks to the team or client. Others talk about valuing the team's victories over individual recognition, but then continue to promote people who steal more than their share of the credit or are constantly seeking the spotlight. These actions send conflicting signals to the team, and people eventually begin to act in whatever way gets them the reward they want.

The simple principle at work is this: whatever you want to see happen at scale, reward it. If you want to see more of a behavior, then structure your incentives around that behavior when it shows up on your dashboard, regardless of whether it registers on your scoreboard. The behaviors you reward are leading indicators of the results you eventually want to see, but you'll only get them if your rewards are predictable, consistent, and substantial.

Predictable: you've talked about the behavior you want and that it will be rewarded. People aren't left guessing as to what you expect from them. There is a clear line between what they do and how they are rewarded.

Consistent: you reward the behavior every single time you see it. Team members don't have to guess whether you truly value the behavior. They see that your actions back up your words when you reward them and their peers for the expected behavior.

Substantial: the reward is something people actually *want*. A $5 coupon to a restaurant on the other side of town isn't an incentive. You have to know your people and understand what motivates them. Make certain that you are effectively incentivizing people to engage in the kinds of behavior you want.

However, not everything is reward worthy. You don't need to incentivize people to do their jobs. That's what their paycheck is for. However, if you see people going out of their way to do something that substantially advances the mission, or you see people taking the kinds of risks that you expect from them even at potential personal cost, these are worth taking note of and calling out publicly, whether in a meeting or with an all-team communication. See these as opportunities to fertilize something that you want to see grow. (However, just because you're fertilizing, don't think you can pile on the BS. It has to be genuine praise.)

Question: How can you better incentivize nonintuitive behaviors that you want to see more of on your team?

FERTILIZE BY LEADING SMALL

"It's not my problem—let someone else handle it."

You'd probably never say those words out loud, but how often do they cross your mind? It's perfectly reasonable to feel that way, especially when you see other people being irresponsible and dropping the ball. After all, why should you have to pick up the pieces after someone else makes a mess? Worse, when you're the only one acting responsibly, and you see other people still receiving accolades and promotions in spite of their shortcomings, it's enough to make you pull your hair out. (That is, if you still have any left.)

Here's the thing: you're right. It's unfair. It's not the way things *should* be. And regardless of all of that, leadership has very little to do with fairness.

Before you can lead big, you must learn to lead small. Recognize that, as a leader, you are also the primary owner of the team's culture. Your credibility is founded upon your willingness to do the little things that other people think are beneath them.

David Wiser, whom we met in chapter 4, is a hiring consultant for some of the largest companies in the world. He helps organizations identify potential new hires, then evaluates them to ensure that they will be a cultural fit and ultimately succeed in their new roles. His twenty-two years in the industry have given him an intimate view of what the most successful leaders do that separates them from the pack—great leaders are willing to do what others simply aren't.

This lesson was reinforced for him when he was vying for a very large, new corporate client and was invited to spend some time with the CEO of the company as part of the vetting process. The lucrative contract was down to just Wiser's company and one other, so the stakes were high. He flew to Salt Lake City to meet with the CEO, who personally met him at the airport to drive him to the corporate headquarters for the meetings with his team. However, upon getting in the car at the airport, the CEO informed him that he needed to stop off at the grocery to pick up a few items and asked if Wiser

Before you can lead big, you must learn to lead small. . . . Your credibility as a leader is founded upon your willingness to do the little things that other people think are beneath them.

would mind accompanying him so they could talk business while they were shopping. Wiser, of course, said it was fine.

They arrived at the grocery store, and the CEO grabbed a cart, which Wiser thought was odd because they were only picking up a few items. Once they had what they needed, which took only a few minutes, they checked out and made their way back to the car. The CEO asked Wiser if he'd mind taking care of the shopping cart while he put the items in the trunk, and again Wiser complied, walking the cart over to the cart corral, which was on the opposite side of the parking lot. "I remember thinking that we couldn't possibly be parked farther from the cart corral," he told me.

As Wiser walked back to the car, he saw the CEO standing there, smiling and extending his hand. "Congratulations, you're hired," he said.

Wiser was stunned. "What? I thought we were on the way to the office to talk that through."

"I know all I need to know." The CEO went on to explain that Wiser's competitor had arrived the day before for the interview and had been through the same scenario, including stopping off at the grocery on the way to the office and being asked to handle the cart. However, the competitor had simply shoved the cart between two cars rather than putting it back where it belonged. "I know that if you're willing to do the right thing in this situation, even when it's really inconvenient, that you'll pay attention to the details when it matters."

Wiser said that this was a reminder to him that these small acts of conscientiousness—like simply making the extra effort to place a shopping cart where it belongs instead of doing the easy or comfortable thing—are markers of good leadership. They show that people actually care not only about themselves and making a good impression, but about how their actions affect those around them, especially people in roles perceived as inferior.

One very simple, small act that leaders can do to reinforce a sense of belonging in a culture, according to Wiser, is to simply seek counsel from the people on their team. "People want to feel valued and heard and utilized," he told me. In his experience, a lot of leaders believe that asking for advice from people on their team is a sign of weakness. But effective leaders don't operate that way. "When talking with people who are leaving their job, I never hear people say 'my boss relies on me too much, or asks my opinion too often.' It's always the opposite. Dissatisfaction is almost always caused by feeling like they're not being listened to or utilized to their full potential." Wiser said that the simple discipline of asking for someone's opinion, and really listening to it, can go a long way toward building team bonds and making people feel like a part of the culture.

Another example of small leadership is owning the appearance of your office environment. Several years ago, I found that the area around the sinks in the restrooms were always covered in pools of water, because water would splash as people washed their hands and reached for paper towels. Because the restrooms were only formally cleaned a few times a day, I assumed the informal role of wiping down the sinks with a few dry paper towels every time I went into the restroom, as a small act of service to everyone else, especially the custodians. (It's a habit that I continue to this day, by the way. I'll often find myself in a restroom just outside an auditorium where I'm

Question: What small actions can you take to model the kind of ownership and culture you desire to see in your team?

about to speak, wiping down the counters and picking up crumpled paper towels off the floor, as audience members step around me, feeling sorry for the obsessive-compulsive guy.) The funny thing is, after I started doing that, I noticed other people starting to do it too, and pretty soon the sinks were no longer covered in pools of water all day. It was a very small act of leadership that—once modeled—became the cultural norm.

Growing and maintaining a great culture takes focus and diligence. Aggressively prune what doesn't belong, and fertilize what you want in abundance. Over time, your culture will take on a life of its own, bearing fruit, much like a well-tended garden.

A great culture doesn't result solely from a great leader, but you cannot maintain a great culture without a great leader. Have the courage to make the hard decisions, to call out deviations and ghost rules, and to lead small so that you gain the trust and respect you need to lead big.

CHECKPOINT

Make bold decisions. A culture is defined by what you say no to as much as by what you say yes to. Here are a few questions, conversations, and rituals to help you aggressively prune and generously fertilize your culture.

Actions

—Identify a few ghost rules and eliminate them. Have a counter-principle that you share whenever the ghost rule comes up in a meeting or conversation.

—Identify areas of "normalization of deviance." Are minor missed deadlines, skipped meetings, or snark creeping into the team's culture? Prune them.

—Identify one of your principles that you're going to focus on this month. Then figure out how you will reward it when you see it. It could even just be a fun prize that someone gets, but it will elevate the principle and help reinforce the culture.

—Find one way to lead small this month. Do something as an act of service to your team.

Conversations

Have a conversation with key team members about the following:

—Are there any ghost rules that you believe are limiting our team's engagement?

—Are there any cultural principles that you don't understand or believe we are not living up to?

—Do you believe that we reward what we say we expect from you, or are we inconsistent?

Rituals

These rituals are also collected at the end of the book under weekly, monthly, and quarterly categories so that you can engage in them regularly.

Weekly: Choose one cultural principle that you will elevate this week. Find ways of working it into your conversation.

Monthly: Consider your team culture and where you need to prune. Are there any deviations from expected behavior that are in danger of becoming normalized?

Quarterly: As you look at your team's upcoming rhythm, consider the cultural principles that you want to elevate and reward over the coming quarter. How will you do so?

CHAPTER 8

STAY ON TARGET

Harnessing Collective Focus

If you don't know where you're going, you might wind up someplace else.

—Yogi Berra

PRINCIPLE: To challenge your team, boldly and effectively channel its collective attention.

FOMO, or the "fear of missing out," is the scourge of many organizations. The fear of missing out on opportunities, ideas, new clients, or a new trend often results in bouncing from shiny object to shiny object and failure to focus. It's one of a leader's primary functions to define what work *truly* matters and what's only a distraction and to narrow the team's gaze to the more urgent and important work at any given moment.

Focus is an act of bravery. To say yes to one thing, you must say no to many, many others. Saying no doesn't win you many friends within the organization, especially when it means killing off pet projects that are important to your boss's boss. Your job is to parse the fake work (false urgencies, side road problems, busywork) from the real work and help your team channel its focus to solving the problems that actually move things forward.

To do this, sharpen your team's sense of focus by clearly and precisely defining the problems it is tasked with solving and establish regular feedback loops to help it stay on target.

BE A LASER, NOT A LIGHTHOUSE

Imagine that you're adrift in an unexplored sea at night without a compass. (Happens to me all the time. You?) Your mission is to get to an island on the far side of the sea and deliver a valuable payload for your employer. However, you have no sense of direction because the night is cloudy—it's pitch black. The only things you can see are a handful of lighthouses on islands throughout the sea, warning you of the dangerous rocks. As you navigate the sea searching for your destination, these lighthouses help you avoid running aground or sideswiping a boulder in the sea, but they don't really tell you how to get to your objective. They are helpful in avoiding failure, but not in achieving success.

Now imagine that your employer has devised an ingenious method for helping you get to your destination. He has secured a very powerful laser, and positioned it at your launch port. He'll point the laser directly at your destination island, so all you have to do is follow it. There's no prescription for the course you take to do so, because as long as you generally follow the laser you'll get where you're going.

I think this is an apt metaphor for the difference between leaders who help their creative team focus and those who actually rob their team of focus. Many leaders operate like a lighthouse, essentially saying "don't go here, and don't go there," but they don't really give their team a clear sense of direction. They adopt a defensive posture that's really more about avoiding bad decisions than it is about making good ones. When a leader assumes a defensive posture, it paralyzes the team. Too many options are worse than too few, because it's hard for the team to know where to begin. A healthy, creative process needs clearly defined boundaries.

I once had a mid-level manager lament to me that it was difficult to get his own manager to commit to a decision on big projects. Instead, the manager wanted to keep his options open as long as possible in case there was a "change in the political winds" and needed to adapt to be more in line with the company's new direction. The unwitting result of this defensive posture was that it paralyzed everyone down the chain and made it impossible for people to do their work. Everything was a last-minute scramble because there was no proactive, decisive action. The leader was acting like a lighthouse.

Instead, function like a laser. Rather than telling the team where *not* to go, lasers give a general direction *to* go. It doesn't prescribe a path, only a destination. There might be many ways to travel and eventually end up where the laser is pointing, but there is no ambiguity about the expected destination.

Do you tend to adopt a *defensive* posture instead of an *offensive* one? Where are you spending energy trying to prevent failure instead of resourcing success?

Your first step in being a laser is to help your team allocate its finite attention to the right problems.

HONE THE FOCUS BY CLEARLY DEFINING YOUR TEAM'S (REAL) WORK

At the heart of all creative work are problems to be solved. How well you define those problems is critical to your team's effectiveness. It's easy to become distracted by attentional vortices, or organizational "attention drains," that draw you away from the main problem. Author Stephen Covey famously quipped, "The main thing is to keep the main thing the main thing."

Focus is about what you *should* be doing, not what you *could* be doing. There are an infinite number of ways your team could spend its finite attention. Creative people are always looking for a problem to solve. They are wired to look for ways to contribute value, and if not given clear direction, they might squander their valuable focus creating wonderful solutions to peripheral problems. If you fail to appropriately challenge them, they may seek challenge in distracting ways. If you provide poor stability, they might be uncertain about which tasks should take the lion's share of their attention at the moment. Your job is to ensure that they understand not only what they *are* doing, but also what they are *not* doing. Here are a few principles for helping you—as the leader—direct your team's gaze.

Define the creative problems you're solving. Not the project you're doing, but the actual *problem* you're solving. If I asked leaders or creative pros what problems they were currently trying to solve, many would have to think for a while before they could respond. This is because we are trained to parse our work into projects or tasks, but we often neglect the much more crucial step of drilling down on what those projects actually *mean*. That's why it's so easy to get distracted by clever, creative ideas that seem worthwhile in the moment but aren't really solving the core problem. When someone is passionate about an idea, it's hard to say no unless you can clearly articulate why it isn't helpful.

At the heart of all creative work are problems to be solved.

For example, right now I'm doing a project called "writing a book," but that's not *really* the problem I'm solving. Rather, the problem I'm solving is: *many creative leaders I meet feel alone, underequipped, and frustrated with their teams.* I've approached this book with the focus on solving that problem. My goal is to *help creative leaders feel understood and valued, equip them with practical tools, and help them get excited about their team's potential.* Every chapter and every decision I make is connected to those three things. I will know that I've succeeded if I've solved that problem effectively and that this is *the* book that is put in every creative leader's hands when he or she takes the reins.

Make certain that every project your team is working on has a clearly defined problem set, and make sure that everyone knows how to know when the problem is solved so that team members don't continue to waste their valuable focus after you've already crossed the finish line. How will you know you're finished? What does success look like? Answering these questions for your team will help people avoid attentional vortices and the temptation to do "just one more thing" after they've already crossed the finish line.

Exercise: For each of the projects you are currently working on, clearly define the core problems you are solving and communicate them concisely to the team.

Refine and assign. Once the problems are clearly defined, ensure that everyone on the team understands clearly who is ultimately tasked with solving each problem and who is *not.* Help team members understand

143

which problems they should devote their finite attention to and which they should let someone else worry about. Don't spread accountability too thin—be precise. Make individuals accountable for specific solutions by defined deadlines.

This is especially important in creative work, because you never really "clock out." Your mind is working 24/7 to develop ideas, sometimes even when you'd rather disengage. By ensuring that each individual clearly understands the problems he is accountable for solving, you limit the amount of wasted time and effort he will spend on things that shouldn't even be on his radar.

Be specific with team members about what you *don't* want them focusing on. Some highly ambitious team members might take it upon themselves to shoulder problems that are really nothing more than a distraction from their core work or are already owned by someone else on the team. In their zeal, they might get sidetracked by an idea or bit of inspiration that adds little real value to the project. Always acknowledge their ideas and enthusiasm, because you want to keep their passion stoked, but redirect their focus on the more important valuable work they should be doing by saying, "I like those ideas a lot, but I'm concerned that they don't perfectly solve the problem. Could we table them, and maybe revisit them for a future project when we have more time to explore them?"

Exercise: Do a quick scan of your team's current projects and ensure that there is clear accountability for every outcome you're trying to achieve.

Tie it back. Finally, always contextualize your team's work by tying everything back to the "main thing." When you're in the fray, it's easy to lose perspective on why the work matters. This doesn't mean that you need to patronize people around you by artificially elevating the importance of their tasks—"Gee, thanks for organizing those files. You've helped us gain a real competitive advantage!"—but make sure that people on your team understand that their role is crucial to the overall focus of the team. Your team members need to know that their work is seen and that it matters.

As discussed earlier, regular "why chats" with your team can help you ensure that people don't get sidetracked or invent false narratives about what's going on. When talking about the work and responsibilities, make certain that individuals know how the work they own plays into the bigger picture of what the team is doing.

HONE THE FOCUS BY ESTABLISHING FEEDBACK LOOPS

In February 2015, a maddening Internet meme spread like wildfire. It was just a simple image—unremarkable in and of itself—of a white and gold dress. The person posting the original image asked a simple question: "What colors are this dress?" with the options "white and gold" or "blue and black." Within a few days, the post had been viewed more than 28 million times as people argued over the true colors of the dress.

In my opinion, anyone looking at the image could clearly see that it was white and gold, but not everyone I knew agreed.

> Be specific with team members about what you *don't* want them focusing on.

In fact, many people who saw the image of the dress swore that it wasn't white and gold, but was instead blue and black. That made no sense to me whatsoever, because the evidence of its white and goldness was right before my eyes. It was plain as day. Anyone who thought otherwise was clearly suffering from some weird form of color blindness or was willfully trying to deceive me.

Except—*except*—the dress was actually blue and black. It wasn't the others who were wrong; it was me. I didn't want to believe it until I saw a picture of the dress taken under different lighting, and lo and behold there it was in all of its obvious blue and blackness. I was stunned. (I wasn't the only one. In an initial poll, over 70 percent of people who saw the original photo believed that the dress was white and gold.)

How could two people looking at the same image come away with two entirely different opinions about something as observable as the color of a dress? It's because each person has a unique perspective, set of experiences, and ingoing filter through which they perceive the stimulus. Some people have more experience looking at objects—for example, dresses—under different lighting conditions and are better able to discern true color even when the ambient light is insufficient. Others, present company included, are just grateful when we somehow manage to make our shirts match our pants in the morning.

Because of vastly different life experiences, each person on your team has a unique perspective. Those experiences create filters that we can't help but bring to the work we do. Two people can look at the same problem and see two entirely different things. This is why we need one another in order to see the full picture. However, it's not as easy as it sounds to gain this perspective. A big part of this process is establishing regular feedback loops with team members so that you can (a) reinforce the "main thing" and (b) hear their frontline perspective on the state of their work.

Allow team members to bring what they're seeing to the table, and tie what they bring to the problems your team is solving. Here are a few questions that you can ask of team members to help this process. Ask these questions in your one-on-ones or in a casual team conversation.

"What do you see that you think others don't?" Or *"What's something obvious that we are missing?"* Ask team members to share something with you that they think is invisible to everyone but them. Team members likely see some problems or dynamics that others don't, but they keep quiet because they don't believe they can share them or fear their perspective is invalid. By giving them permission to speak those things, you lessen the chances of tripping over something that should have been obvious but that no one was talking about.

"What worries you about this project?" Sometimes, people on the front lines have a much better sense than you do of ways in which the team is getting distracted, but they may not be talking about it. Giving them permission to speak hard truths can help you identify potential problems and areas where your focus is misaligned.

"What opportunities aren't we exploring?" By simply asking people to share the patterns they are seeing or the potential unexplored opportunities within a project, you're leveraging their "on the ground" perspective to open up new areas of potential action for the team. Plus, you get the added benefit of using this question to vet potential leadership ability of the people on your team. If you find that someone routinely comes to you with great ideas or opportunities that no one else has offered, it shows you that he could have leadership potential.

"Where are we getting off track?" Give your team members permission to tell you where they perceive that you've lost your focus or

are working on ancillary issues that aren't helping you make progress. This accomplishes a few things. First, it illuminates areas where the team perceives a misalignment of values and actions, and it gives you a chance to clarify. Second, it helps you see areas where the team's focus is softening. It's hard for your team members to get too far off track if you are having these regular alignment conversations with them.

"What's the best thing we're doing right now?" Ask for perspective on what the team is doing especially well and where your team members think that they are really creating a lot of value for your stakeholders. There could be things happening that you are either unaware of or that you didn't realize were important to people on the front lines. Give them a chance to champion the things that excite them.

Of course, don't sneak up on someone and just spout off: "Hey, Jill! What opportunities aren't we exploring right now?" The conversations need to happen within a context of trust and safety so that team members feel permission to speak freely and fully. That's the only way you can be certain that you're getting their full perspective— good, bad, and ugly.

HONE THE FOCUS BY *ALWAYS* ACHIEVING COMPLETION IN CONVERSATIONS

An unbelievable amount of focus, time, and energy is spent in many organizations relitigating decisions that have already been made and should have been final. Not only is this a massive sinkhole for the team's resources, it's a drain on its emotional engagement and a drag on its sense of mission. It can also cause constant questioning of your leadership. The main contributors to this relitigation are twofold:

incomplete conversations and unclear authority. Both eat away at your team's ability to focus clearly.

> **Give [team members] a chance to champion the things that excite them.**

Actually end your conversations. Don't allow a conversation to end before it's agreed by everyone that the conversation is complete and all parties have a clear understanding of the outcome. A lack of finality in conversations kills focus. Just because something is resolved in your mind doesn't mean that it's resolved to your team.

There are a number of reasons why you might end a conversation prematurely:

You've said your piece, and you assume that everyone is on the same page.

The conversation gets awkward, and you don't want to deal with the emotional work necessary to resolve it. You look for the first way out.

You are unexpectedly interrupted by another demand and aren't able to finish, so you just quickly jump to the end without laying the appropriate groundwork for understanding.

You don't fully say everything you want to say because you are afraid of how it will be received.

Any of these situations could result in someone leaving the meeting unclear and unfocused. What does this mean?

You'll have to schedule another conversation just to clarify the first one, which means you'll probably have to relitigate the entire situation.

The circumstances will possibly change in the interim, and there's a chance that you'll need to rethink your decision, which requires even *more* of your team's focus and energy.

In the time between the two meetings, spinoff conversations will occur as people try to sort out their own thoughts about the matter, all the while hoping to curry enough support to influence your decision, which isn't yet final.

Any and all of these situations is an utter waste of resources. Always complete your conversations and make certain your team member has what she needs before moving on. A great way to do this is to simply ask: "Is there anything else you need from me right now to get moving on this?"

Establish clear authority and submit to your own decisions. In the book *Principles*, Bridgewater founder Ray Dalio wrote, "Make sure that people don't confuse their right to complain, give advice, and debate with the right to make decisions." Although you want to create a culture of transparency and contribution, you also want to ensure that everyone understands that there will be a decision at the end, and they may not like it. Just because team members have the right to offer input doesn't mean that they have earned the right to make the final decision. It's important to help people on your team understand the difference between permission and authority.

This can be a confusing point to many people, especially those early in their career. They think that permission to give input means that they are on equal footing with the decision makers. They get frustrated when their opinion is invited but not used. Proximity to power isn't power, so clarify who will be making the end decision and how that decision will be made. This will prevent a lot of headaches in the end, when there is disagreement about the final decision.

This, by the way, also applies to you as the team leader. If you have handed over responsibility for a project to someone on your team, you are submitting to his or her decision-making authority. If you regularly step in and override people on your team after you've handed them responsibility for a decision, you will lose their trust.

Here are a few questions to ask yourself about whether you are creating clear lines of authority on your team:

Just because team members have the right to offer input doesn't mean that they have earned the right to make the final decision. It's important to help people on your team understand the difference between permission and authority.

As you consider the key projects you are working on, is it clear to everyone who has decision-making authority and who is merely a contributor?

Are the decision-making criteria clear to everyone on the team so that there is no ambiguity about how and when the final decisions will be made?

Is anyone waiting on you in order to make their decision? If so, how can you free them up, whether that means getting them the information they need or giving them permission to take the next step with your full blessing?

HONE THE FOCUS BY KILLING ASSUMPTIONS

Have you ever had the sense, as you were talking with a coworker, that even though you were talking about a project familiar to both of you, you were speaking different languages? You suddenly realized in that moment that although you thought you were aligned, you each had a very different understanding of what was actually happening with the project or client.

It's crazy, but this happens all the time. You assume that you and your fellow team members are all on the same page because you're privy to all of the same information, but how that information is absorbed and interpreted is a very personal thing and can lead to sharp division if you don't seek common understanding.

Here are a few quick ways to identify any focus-stealing assumptions:

Immediately note and question any perceived misunderstandings. It's easy to gloss over an errant comment in a meeting as meaningless, but often it's a signal of a deeper misunderstanding. In a courteous and sincere way, ask your team member what she meant by her statement or what she was thinking when she took a particular action. It's better to have that uncomfortable conversation now than to have to take massive, corrective action later.

Regularly scan your own thinking for possible assumptions. We live by assumptions. Our brains don't have the capacity to process every situation as if it were new, so we've developed a system of predictions about what will and won't happen next. Some of those assumptions are probably valid (gravity will continue to operate as it did yesterday), and some might be invalid (our clients want today what they wanted yesterday, or my relationship with my peer is fine). It helps to regularly scan for potential areas of assumption or misalignment. As a part of your weekly checkpoint, ask, "What might I be assuming to be true?" and "What might I be assuming to be false?" Then ask, "What if that were not the case?"

Take five minutes now to save five hours later. At the end of each meeting, take five minutes to clarify objectives, talk specific next actions and accountability, and ensure that there is common alignment. Also, to the best of your ability, attempt to foster an environment in which others are able to ask questions without fear of reprisal. Put your gun away. Remember, only one person survives a gunfight.

We all depend upon others in order to do our best work. Don't allow your misplaced assumptions to drive a wedge between you and your peers.

HONE THE FOCUS BY MAKING THE SCOREBOARD PUBLIC

If you walk into a sporting event in the middle of the game, the first thing you do is look at the scoreboard. You do this because you want to have some context for what's going on in the game, how much time is left, and maybe even who you should root for. It's really difficult to be engaged when you don't know the score.

The same principle applies to your team's work. It's hard for team members to feel engaged and invested in the work when they are uncertain whether their efforts are making a difference and whether they are "winning." The first step in helping your team understand how what they are doing is affecting the work is to make the scoreboard public.

This week: What will constitute success for your team's efforts over the next handful of days? What specific outcomes do you hope to have achieved?

This quarter: What are the big initiatives that you're tracking and that will constitute the score for this quarter? Make sure that your team has a clear understanding of the larger scoreboard and how you are marking success or failure over the coming few months.

Why not "this year"? Although many teams have yearly marks they are trying to hit, I often find that horizon is simply too long. Instead, I'd encourage you to break those long-arc objectives into smaller ones that are more easily trackable for the team. For example, if you are responsible for leading a major rebranding effort for your organization this year, you might want to consider breaking that into smaller and more "scorable" projects that help your team stay focused and motivated rather than feeling that there is still so much work ahead of them.

Make certain that your scoreboard is concrete, public, and accessible to the team. This could mean writing your team's objectives on a whiteboard in a public place or creating an index card–sized printout of objectives for them to keep in their workspace. However you do it, keep the scoreboard in front of them so that they know what you are measuring. And once you make the scoreboard public, never

> **It's hard for team members to feel engaged and invested in the work when they are uncertain whether their efforts are making a difference and whether they are "winning."**

> *Question: What is on your scoreboard today, this week, and this quarter, and how might you share it with your team in a public way?*

keep score in a way that's inconsistent with that scoreboard. If your team senses that your actions aren't lining up with what you say you're measuring, then they will ignore your words and do whatever gets them the recognition or rewards they desire.

How your team allocates its finite attention is a significant contributing factor to its success. This all begins with a leader who is able and willing to make difficult choices and prune unnecessary distractions so that the team can confidently get to work on what matters most.

Of course, a big element of your team's ability to focus effectively is whether it has the collective energy to apply to the work. In the next chapter, we'll address how to manage your team's energy and use "white space" to unleash brilliance.

CHECKPOINT

Lead your team by allocating its finite attention to the main mission. Here are a few ways to do so:

Actions

—List every project your team is working on, and define the core problem that it's solving. Then write a one-sentence problem statement that clearly articulates what the team is trying to accomplish. Share it with the team.

—Make the scoreboard public. Make sure that everyone knows how you will define success over the coming week, month, and quarter.

Conversations

Have a conversation with key team members about the following:

—Is there any place where you're confused about our objectives?

—What opportunities do you see that we aren't exploring?

—Is there anything you're being asked to do and can't understand why?

Rituals

These rituals are also collected at the end of the book under weekly, monthly, and quarterly categories so that you can engage in them regularly.

Weekly: Consider each member of your team and the problems he or she is tasked with solving. Are the problems clearly defined?

Monthly: Consider the upcoming projects your team will be working on and establish clear challenges (problem statements) for each.

Quarterly: Take time to think about areas of potential misalignment or assumptive behavior on your team. Are you sensing a growing gap between the *what* and the *why* of your work?

CHAPTER 9

DEFEND THEIR SPACE

Managing Your Team's Margin

We have so much time and so little to do. No! Wait! Strike
that! Reverse it!

—Willy Wonka

**PRINCIPLE: To create stability, manage your team's margin by
aggressively protecting "white space."**

Quick: count from one to twenty. And while you're doing it, I want
you to solve the following math problem: 420 ÷ 5.

Unless you're a savant, you would probably find it difficult to
accomplish both tasks simultaneously. That's because the executive
function of your mind is only able to fully engage in one task at a
time. You might be able to switch rapidly back and forth between
tasks and accomplish both, but you cannot actually *do* both at the
same time.

Many organizations value efficiency over every other indicator
of productivity. That's because efficiency can be measured. You
know exactly how many sales you made in a given time period, how

many projects you completed, or how many meetings you held. Because of this, organizations are in a constant chase to do more with less, stacking meeting after meeting and piling more work on top of their most capable and proven workers. In doing so, they find that their chase after efficiency only burns out their top players and demotivates everyone else, resulting in the opposite of what they had hoped to achieve.

Brilliant ideas emerge in the white space. They happen when you and your team are able to step back, spot patterns, and make connections that might otherwise go overlooked because of the overwhelming pressures of the create-on-demand world. However, many teams miss the best ideas because they lack the margin to think deeply about the work and make intuitive leaps and connections.

To help your creative team unleash its brilliance, you need to protect its margin. This doesn't mean allowing the team to slack off or intentionally underperform but rather ensuring that your team has the space that it needs to go beyond surface (or first-order) ideas and get to deeper, more valuable thoughts and ideas.

You probably have a good grasp of where your team is spending its time. In fact, there are more tools for managing time than at any point in human history. However, you may not have a true grasp of your team's most invisible yet powerful resource: its energy. To be a great leader, you need to move beyond just managing your team's time. Instead, be conscious of how your decisions about priorities, schedule, systems, and expectations affect your team's energy and how—as the leader—you have tremendous power to be either an energy giver or an energy vampire.

Innovation and creative breakthrough often happen in the white space, when your team is able to step back, process, play with ideas, and experiment. When there is no margin, there is no room for experimentation or deep thought.

Expectation escalation can suffocate your team and prevent it from performing at its best. There is a fine line between challenging people to bring their best work to the table and stretching them beyond the bounds of reason. Worse, if you treat your team like a machine, that's exactly what it will become. It will crank out predictable, uninspired work.

Stand your ground when guarding your team's margin. Refuse to allow the steady ratcheting up of organizational demands, such as meetings, incremental projects, or side work, to rob your team of its critical energy. Just because there is empty time on the calendar, it doesn't mean that that time is truly *available*. Filling every spare space in your team's work life is a guaranteed way to squelch its creativity. In order to prevent expectation escalation from stifling your team's performance, protect it from the onslaught of organizational demands that eat up the margin of most creative pros. The best creative leaders are freedom fighters.

YOU, THE FREEDOM FIGHTER

No matter how effective you are at managing your own expectations of the team, you can't always control expectations that come from on high. In a previous role, Josh Banko was a product designer at Apple, where he led many great product design teams within the Macintosh and iPad groups over thirteen years. Five of those years were spent architecting and leading the original iPad team from concept to launch of the product. As a team lead, Banko says that one of his main roles was to create the space in which his team could do

If you treat your team like a machine, that's exactly what it will become. It will crank out predictable, uninspired work.

its best work, which often meant fending off requests from above so that they didn't create unnecessary pressure: "You can't just say no, because then you'll be forced to do it anyway and won't have a choice about how to do it."

Instead of just saying no, Banko says that he tries to "assess the *why* behind the request." It's sometimes the case that people are asking for things for which they don't understand the implications to the team's focus and energy. Some leaders jump whenever they are asked to do something, because they want to please their own manager. However, this can create a culture of unpredictability and burnout. Assume the role of protector and freedom fighter for your team. Banko told me, "Try to create a little bit of buffer so that you're not putting your team against impossible odds when something unexpectedly comes up."

Anyone can say yes. It feels good because it seems like progress is being made, even if only because everyone is agreeing on something. However, the art of leadership is the art of learning how to say no. It takes courage to fight for your team's freedom.

It's easy to say no to the obvious time and energy wasters, but it's much more difficult to do so when something has some degree of value. When a task, project, or meeting is important to *someone, somewhere*, it can be a tall order to prune it. This is the role of the leader.

Sometimes, very good ideas have to die so that something better can be born.

Start cutting unnecessary responsibilities and commitments from your team's schedule so that they have the margin needed to deliver their best synthesis and effort. Begin by building "buffers" against the onslaught of expectations and information that can overload your team. The buffers are rules, systems, or rituals that provide a bit of protected "white space" for your team and prevent people from filling their time and attention up to the max.

There are two major areas where you need to focus on building buffers for your team: attention and time.

BUILD ATTENTIONAL BUFFERS

We are simply overwhelmed with new information every single day, and making sense of it all is an impossible feat. A 2009 study from the University of California, San Diego, revealed that the average American consumes around thirty-four gigabytes of data and over a hundred thousand words each day. The study found that the amount of information processed each day increased 350 percent between 1980 and 2008. There is no question that we are swimming in data and information, but winnowing that information down to the most actionable pieces is a challenge. Because of your role, you are uniquely positioned to protect your team from the noise by building attentional buffers that protect them from needless distraction.

The art of leadership is the art of learning how to say no.

Attentional buffers are like gates in the wall that only allow important information through to the team. They protect your team from the onslaught of (sometimes irrelevant) information that is a part of organizational life and allow people to instead focus on relevant data that will help them deliver value. More information is not better. Better information is better. *Selective* information is best.

Here are a few strategies for building buffers around your team's attention:

Stop copying me. It seems like an obvious question, but it needs to be asked: Do you *really* need to "CC" everyone on the team on that announcement? Often, people are copied on e-mails not because they are expected to do anything with the information, but as an insurance policy for the sender. ("What? I sent you the e-mail about that.") However, with each e-mail, the recipient must (a) decide whether it's relevant to her, (b) decide whether any action is necessary on her part, and (c) either archive the e-mail in case it is needed later or (most likely) delete it. Although it seems like no big deal, it can actually be a major drain on the white space of the team because every e-mail requires each team member to go through that process, even if it's largely irrelevant to the person's own work.

Because e-mail is free to send, we forget that it can be costly. A marginally relevant e-mail can prevent your team from focusing deeply on the truly important issues.

We sometimes think that we're being inclusive by copying everyone on our communications, but all we're really doing is increasing the likelihood people will miss (or ignore) something that really matters. Consider how much money is wasted by the organization in paying people to review and delete unnecessary communications. Further, not only do your e-mails directly affect everyone on your team, remember that how you treat e-mail (as a leader) communicates the expected behavior for the rest of the team.

As a first step in building an attentional buffer, consider limiting your e-mail communications to the team to only those that are necessary, and always consider who needs to be copied on an e-mail before sending. Protect your team from the tyranny of the inbox.

Limit the project horizon. You will necessarily have a longer perspective on the work than your team does. As such, you probably know much more about what's coming next month or next quarter than the members of your team. However, just because you know something is coming in a few months doesn't mean that this information needs to be passed directly to them. Be protective of what information you pass along to your team and when so that your team doesn't have to focus on things it can do nothing about at the moment.

In a busy season, before you pass along information to your team about upcoming work or organizational initiatives, ask, "Can we really do anything with this information right now?" and "Is this information useful in any unique way right now?" If the answer is no, then it might be better to hold it off until it's actually relevant.

Necessary meetings, necessary people. *Why are all of these people here?* Allie thought. She was a writer tasked with generating content for a branding initiative newsletter, and she was sitting in a room with no fewer than a dozen people, all of whom were there to weigh in on what should go into the next issue. "Everyone who was even marginally connected to the project was there," Allie told me. "If there was any chance they might have value to add, they were invited." The problem was that—with all of those voices in the room and precious little time to hear from them all—very few decisions were actually made. Instead, Allie and her team often had to do the bulk of the work on the back end to figure out what was best for the newsletter.

Similar to copying everyone on an e-mail in order to "cover" themselves, many leaders invite to a meeting everyone who might have even a marginal interest in a project. Although there are certainly times to err on the side of inclusion, most meetings don't qualify. Instead, commit to only having necessary meetings with necessary people. Whenever you are scheduling a meeting, consider: "What outcome must we achieve by the end?" and "Who absolutely needs to be there in order to achieve it?" Just answering these two questions will help you avoid taxing your team's precious energy with needless meetings. Josh Banko told me, "I want my time to be respected and I try to model that for my team. Really assess the value of your role in a meeting and try to find ways of adding that value prior to the meeting. I never have meetings that last longer than thirty minutes, and I always publish the agenda ahead of time."

Additionally, you may want to have a frank conversation with team members about their involvement in recurring meetings. Ask them whether they think their presence is necessary, or whether they can pass along any critical information to someone else whose involvement is more necessary. There's no reason for someone to spend an hour in a meeting just for the five minutes that are actually relevant to her work.

Because e-mail is free to send, we forget that it can be costly.

All of these strategies protect the attentional margin of your team, which is often eaten up by ancillary communication, meetings, and commitments. By eliminating these attention- and energy-wasting activities, you are fighting for your team's freedom and clearing the path for it to do its best work.

BUILD TIME BUFFERS

"I just have no margin at all," a marketing firm employee told me. "I spend much of my day running from meeting to meeting, some of which overlap, and I often feel like I'm playing catch-up." She told me that it seems like the better she performs, the more responsibility she's given, which means more meetings. The net effect is that she's being asked to do more with less time and less ability to focus, because she's constantly juggling her calendar.

This is not an uncommon phenomenon. Another person put it more bluntly: "Meetings are the scourge of our organization." Meetings are necessary to a healthy team, but when you spend most of your day in meetings, it makes it challenging to accomplish any of the real work for which you're accountable. Worse, when meetings are stacked one after the other, it sometimes means little time to think or be strategic about them. You're simply being reactive.

You are uniquely positioned to help the team avoid "meeting pinball," just bouncing between meetings all day in reactive mode. One strategy to implement to help your team better manage its energy is to establish buffers between tasks or events that allow your team to reset, consider what's next, and catch its breath between commitments. Rather than stacking commitments back to back, you are giving each commitment that you schedule the amount of time it needs and no more, and you're ensuring that every commitment has a little breathing room blocked off around it so that there is margin for participants.

It's careless to waste someone's time. When you do, you are essentially wasting the person's life. It's not like we wake up in the morning, thinking, *I wonder how I can turn our day into a wasteland of meaningless activity and fruitless meetings.* No, it happens via little decisions over time. What you model is what you get, and if you model for your team that you don't truly value its time, then it will reciprocate. You will soon find that your unhealthy use of time has infiltrated the entire organization and set the tone for how work gets done.

Build buffers between scheduled meetings. If you truly want the people on your team to bring their best thinking to a meeting, don't chain meetings back to back, especially if they are about different projects. Give them five or ten minutes to recollect themselves between meetings, to check in with their other commitments if necessary, and to refocus on the next topic.

Who decided that meetings should be an hour by default? Is it the calendar program that your company uses? I encourage you to consider changing the default meeting expectation for your team. Instead of defaulting to an hour just because that's what most people or teams do, make it forty minutes. Or make it a half hour. Better yet, make each meeting precisely as long as it needs to be to finish the conversation.

My friend riCardo Crespo, who has held global executive creative director roles at major companies, such as 20th Century Fox and Mattel, once told me that he would host *standing meetings*, which were designed to take as little time as needed while still being productive. Rather than inviting people to his office for a "formal" sit-down conversation, he was known to say something like, "Meet me at the potted plant on the northwest corner on the eighth floor at 9:20 a.m. tomorrow morning." He knew that by choosing an informal setting (outside the formality of sitting in a boardroom or office), no one would settle in for a long and winding conversation. Instead, there would be an urgency to get to the heart of the matter quickly so that everyone could move on with their day. He would come to this five- to ten-minute standing meeting fully informed and prepared to discuss the topic; then each person would move on with their day.

Although you don't have to be as prescriptive as that, I'd encourage you to infuse specificity into how you schedule meetings and make them only as long as they need to be in order to accomplish their objective. Exercising precision in how you schedule and run your meetings communicates that you value your team's time. (And, frankly, your own as well.) Here are a few additional thoughts about meetings that will help you honor your team's most valuable finite resource:

1. **Only call a meeting with a specific purpose and desired outcome.** *Never* call a speculative meeting. The only reason that you should call a meeting is when you need a specific group of people to weigh in on a decision, and the outcome is clearly defined. Some leaders call a meeting as a way to soothe their own anxiety. They want to assure themselves that progress is being made. This is terribly demotivating to the team, which must break from its tasks in order to meet.

2. **Make sure that everyone knows the purpose or outcome, and assign each person prework before the meeting.** It should be clear to all attendees why you are meeting and what you are planning to accomplish. In addition, they should understand what they're accountable for bringing to the meeting, whether it's ideas, an update on progress, or a specific question that they need answered. Give them plenty of time to pull together what they need. No one should come to the meeting unprepared, ever.

3. **Set only as much time as is necessary to accomplish the objective.** As I said before: *do not default to sixty-minute meetings.* I can't make this any more clear. Schedule as much time as you think you'll need to accomplish the objective, and no more. It

sends a powerful signal to your team that you value its time, and it also encourages everyone to use the time wisely, as there is little margin for banter.

4. **Start and end on time.** This one needs little explanation. You can say whatever you want about how much you value people's time, but your actions prove your words. Be a person of integrity and honor, and expect others to follow suit. Refuse to tolerate those who waste your time or the time of others.

5. **Save the small talk for lunch or the elevator.** Meetings are for getting things done, not for catching up on the family or talking about the big game last night. Welcome everyone and get right to the point. Although you may think that this makes you a cold, distant leader, people will actually love you more for respecting their time.

6. **At the end of the meeting, assign next actions and ensure that accountability is clear.** End your meeting by reiterating the decision that was made, offering everyone a last chance to speak up about it, and then assigning clear next steps and accountability for action. It should be crystal clear who will do what and by when.

7. **Take accountability when things go off the rails.** Inevitably, there will be a meeting that doesn't go as planned. There is a surprise issue, or the conversation becomes more complicated than initially expected. You still need to respect people's time. Give them the option of extending the meeting to a specific time to allow more discussion or setting a separate meeting

time to finish the conversation. Don't assume that you can just continue the meeting without first getting people's permission. Remember that time spent in a meeting is time *not* spent creating value for the organization. Everyone in your meeting has a lot of work waiting for them at their desk, and that work isn't going to do itself.

8. **Eliminate recurring meetings unless they are absolutely necessary.** When you have a problem to solve, it's easy to default to calling a meeting. Subsequently, it's easy to establish a recurring meeting as a way to touch base on a regular basis. These recurring meetings might be valuable for a while, but they often outlive their usefulness quickly. Don't set a recurring commitment on the calendar unless it meets all of the criteria of having a specific and imminent outcome. And if you have any recurring meetings on the calendar, check them against these criteria and prune if necessary.

Of course, all of this is just good, simple meeting hygiene, but it's often not practiced because we get busy and overwhelmed. Set the tone for how other people's meetings operate within your organization, then be very careful about how you manage your own.

Exercise: Evaluate your current slate of recurring meetings and consider eliminating or adapting them to better honor your team's time. (And your own.)

Question: How can you better structure your current meeting schedule so that there is less wasted time and energy and more white space for your team to recollect and refocus on the work?

Question: Are there any commitments or expectations that bookend your team's day that need to be adjusted so that they have more margin around the edges of their schedule?

Articulate these expectations to the people on your team so that they understand how much you value their time. And your own.

Build buffers at the beginning and end of the day. Similarly, consider how your team begins and ends its day. Do you schedule meetings at the very beginning or the very end of the day, causing your team to come screaming into work with little time to adjust, and then whimpering out at the end of the day, with nothing left in the tank? Understandably, there are some situations that call for meetings to be scheduled first or last in the day, but I encourage you to limit them as much as you can. By doing so, you'll allow your team members to settle in, prepare, and bring their full attention and energy to the matters at hand. Also, you'll allow them to wrap up any important matters at the end of the day before going home so that they can be refreshed and ready to go the following morning.

Establish "no-fly zone" time. One of the most challenging things about creative work, in which a lot of deep thought time is required to deliver value, is the constant interruptions. It's difficult to really focus on the work that you're doing when there is constant pinging from others, including, but not exclusive to, e-mails, text messages, instant messages, and stop-bys for "just a quick question." Just as you're really starting to gain traction on something, you have to come back up to the surface to address an urgent (or not-so-urgent) interruption.

One team I encountered had taken a novel approach to this

problem. They established what was called no-fly zone time for their creative workers, between the hours of 11 a.m. and 1 p.m. This meant that you were under organizational orders *not* to interrupt people in the middle of their work unless they expressly signaled it was OK. (Typically, the default is to interrupt unless told not to. This team had reversed the expectation and stated that the default was *not* to interrupt unless given explicit permission.) By doing this, the team had marked off a period of time each day when team members knew that they would have predictable time to focus and dive deep on the creative problems they were trying to solve, but also to simply breathe and listen to their intuition without the constant bombardment of stimuli.

Creative work requires protected time. However, there is never a guaranteed result for your effort. Therefore, it's always easier to gravitate toward the work that feels like it's getting you somewhere, even if that means avoiding the much more challenging (but valuable) work that might actually make an impact. Worse, as a leader it's easy to unknowingly create a culture in which you reward "fake work," or all of the administrative but relatively low-value activities that your team does, and unwittingly downplay the "real work," the work that requires intense periods of focused and skilled effort.

Professor Cal Newport coined a phrase for this intense, focused activity: "deep work." He separates it from "shallow work," which is the kind of work that feels immediately productive but isn't actually all that valuable, and he argues that the ability to do deep work is the single most valuable critical skill that creative pros must develop in order to succeed in today's marketplace. He also believes that a creative pro who is prone to digital distractions—such as Facebook and Twitter—is like an Olympic sprinter who takes up smoking. It just doesn't make any sense to create space in your life for something that is only designed to distract you from the important work that you want to do. Deep work is what allows you to go beyond the most obvious answer and bring deeper, more systemic thinking to your team's complex problems. Expecting your team to provide brilliant results without giving it the permission and time to engage in deep work is like asking a writer to compose a book while depriving him of the backspace key.

The first thing that Newport says you must do in order to work deeply is to set specific time blocks on your calendar for the work that requires special focus (for example, institutionalized no-fly zone time). Without these dedicated time blocks, you are perpetually prone to interruption and are less likely to achieve breakthroughs when none are obvious. Encourage your team to set aside blocks of time each week to work—without interruption—on its most important problems. And, more important, honor the boundaries that your team members have set around this deep work time. Make an appointment on your calendar for your deep work time, and honor it just like you would a meeting with someone else.

Some of your team members won't intuitively ask for this time, because (a) most cultures don't embrace this "deep work" mind-set, and (b) they may be unaware that there is an entirely new level to which they can take the work if they embrace it. Give your team explicit permission to establish deep work time throughout the course of the week.

Next, choose a specific problem to work on during your deep work time. Again, this isn't time set aside to "crank through" your e-mail or to fill out reports. This is work in which you are bringing unique expertise and focused creative thought to add unique value. Encourage your team to prioritize its most important, unsolved creative problem or the work that really needs to make significant progress, and have team members schedule an appointment with themselves to work on it. Again, this isn't the same thing as retreating to your cubicle and half working while occasionally checking your e-mail. You need to be deeply concentrating on the problem you're solving and clearly focused on the outcome you're trying to achieve.

Finally, find a place to go where you won't be interrupted. You need to send a signal to the entire team that you are not reachable. And give your team permission to do the same. Again, if deep work time isn't protected, your team will stop practicing it. Turn off your phone and e-mail and anything else that might interrupt your thinking. Put on noise-canceling headphones if it's helpful. Environment is important, so do whatever is necessary to help you get into a state of deep focus.

Here's the challenging thing for many leaders: deep work is risky. There are no guarantees that the few hours your team members spend in deep, focused work will actually produce the results they want, and that can be daunting to them and difficult for you to justify to your own manager. That's why it's much easier for many leaders to gravitate toward quick answers and more productive-feeling, shallow work. However, if you want brilliant results, you must be willing to assume the risk.

Question: How might you establish a block of time in the day (or at least a few times per week) when everyone can have predictable, uninterruptible time for deep focus and clear thinking?

HAVE A "BREAK THE GLASS" STRATEGY

In most buildings you'll see fire extinguishers positioned in the wall in the event of a fire. They are typically encased behind glass with the instructions "In case of emergency, break glass" printed boldly over it. While these extinguishers are rarely used, their presence is necessary in case of an unexpected fire.

In creative work, it's helpful to have a "break the glass" strategy as a plan B in the event of an unexpected emergency. This could mean a sudden change of strategy, or a mandate from on high, or something that your team hasn't allocated resources toward but is suddenly of critical importance to the organization.

When possible, you should plan for any of these contingencies ahead of time so that you aren't scrambling in the moment to try to make things work. You don't want these last-minute situations to become such a significant burden on the team that it causes burnout and begins to affect the other important work that it's charged with doing. You don't have to think of everything that could go wrong, but should instead have a blanket plan for dealing with curveballs that are tossed your way.

A good break the glass strategy has four components:

—*Who will do the work?* Will you pull people from existing projects in order to work on the emergency, or will you bring in people from the outside? How many people are you prepared to use, and for how long? If you're bringing in people from outside your team, where will these people come from?

—*How will it be funded?* Even though you may not need it, always, always, always ask for money to be budgeted for your break the glass strategy. You should be ready to pull the trigger at a moment's notice without needing to haggle over which line item the resources will come from. Also, never, never, never use your break the glass funds for anything other than an emergency. Don't rob the storehouse for a snack only to starve during the zombie apocalypse.

—*How long will it last?* If something is more seasonal than short term, then it's not really an emergency, it's a new expectation. Refrain from allowing seasonal emergencies to become long-term expectations for those you report to. Once they see that you're able to make things happen quickly in a pinch, it will be tempting to rely on that instead of planning thoroughly. Make certain when you employ the break the glass strategy to let everyone know that this is a unique and rare circumstance, that it's for only a season, and that it likely won't happen again for a while.

—*What are we willing to compromise?* Finally, discuss in advance what you're willing to compromise in order to make your emergency strategy work. Everything is a trade-off. It's possible that something else will need to suffer, at least a little and for a while, in order to deal with the emergency situation. Before you start juggling, have a frank and concrete discussion with the team and with your own manager about which balls you're willing to let drop so that you can accomplish the overall mission of the moment.

Answering each of these questions in advance will help you avoid the pain of having to negotiate in the heat of the moment, thus losing precious focus, time, and energy trying to figure out how you're going to make it all happen. It's always far better to have a plan for dealing with a fire than to run around searching for a fire extinguisher while the building is burning down around you.

However, please note that your break the glass strategy is not something that should be used unless absolutely necessary. If you're replacing extinguishers every day, you need to have a different conversation with your own leader about their arson problem. As one leader told me, "One of these days, I hope to get around to the work that I'm actually supposed to be doing instead of just putting out fires all the time." When this is the environment you operate in, your team will struggle to establish rhythm and you'll eventually burn out. You must have some measure of predictability if you truly want your team to settle into the flow and produce its best work.

MEASURE PRODUCTIVITY IN INTERVALS, NOT SNAPSHOTS

In creative work, input does not equal output. You cannot reasonably expect that two people, given the same amount of time, resources, and direction, will produce equally great work every time. It might take one person a little longer to solve a problem, whereas another might solve it in a flash and to a different caliber. Similarly, you cannot expect that a person will produce consistent results over a long period of time based upon the results of one project. Creativity has an ebb and flow to it, and you must account for that when you set expectations for your team.

If you treat your team like a machine, it will begin to produce like one: mechanical, expected, and no more than asked. However, to produce great results that exceed expectations, build a culture that measures value, not time. Your team is not paid to show up and punch a clock every day. Team members are paid for the unique value and skills they bring to the work. Everyone knows this, but it's often not how we actually measure and reward their efforts.

Many organizations practice "snapshot productivity," meaning that they informally measure an individual's productivity based upon a snapshot in time—such as how they performed on one project or task—rather than over a period of time. When this happens, it places a lot of emphasis on what someone has done lately rather than on the total value they are producing for the team over time. However, all creative professionals experience natural peaks and troughs of productive output over time, Snapshot productivity fails to take this reality into account.

One leader told me that she was almost to the point of firing an employee because of a few recent projects. Then, upon taking a closer look at the work, she realized that he had actually been one of the more productive team members over a longer period of time. He was simply burned out from a season of especially challenging work that required a lot of late nights and even weekends, and he was not back to full strength yet. It's natural to expect peak performance at all times, but it's simply not realistic.

To optimize long-term value, allow your team the space and freedom to dive deep into its work, to have some margin to play with ideas and seek beyond the first answer, and to bring fresh synthesis to the conversation. Then you will find that the value you produce is far greater, and your team will feel energized and invested in the work. To do this, you need to think about your time not in terms of "do we physically have the time to do this?" but instead in terms of "how can we use our time and resources to set the team up to produce maximum value?"

Question: Are you measuring your team's output by its efficiency rather than by the value it's creating? How can you adjust your expectations so that you aren't treating your team like a machine?

HOW TO NEGOTIATE FOR WHITE SPACE

Creating margin for your team sounds great in theory, but there are a lot of practical considerations that can be tricky to navigate. Your organization is wired to squeeze as much productivity out of the team as possible, and it will take some negotiation on your part to protect your team from the onslaught of expectations and information that are a regular part of organizational life. Manage up so that your own leader understands why you are trying to protect your team.

Explain the *why* behind your method. Help your leader understand that you are trying to manage your team's collective energy in order to help people bring their best efforts to the work that matters most. As a result, you're trying to limit unnecessary time and attention drains so that they can have the space they need to create the value they were hired for. (Imagine that—giving people the space they need to do great work. What a novel concept!) Although it's likely you'll get approval when you have this conversation, it's also likely that you'll have to continually fight encroachment on multiple fronts. When something is critical to the organization, it suddenly becomes an emergency to everyone. By having this conversation with your leader early in the process, you are laying the foundation for difficult decisions you may need to make later.

> Protect your team's energy, because without it, [the team] will produce little value.

Ask to be the filter for time and attention requests. Although you can control the commitments you ask your team to make, you can't control people who go around you to get to your team. Ask your leader and your peers to connect with you before asking your team for something. Yes, it's an annoying speed bump in the process, but it helps you better track what's being asked of your team and also allows you to protect your team from unnecessary requests that are better handled elsewhere.

Regularly share the results of your strategy. If someone on your team had a great idea during a bit of focused downtime, make sure to share that with your leader and peers so that they can see the results of your "white space" effort. This isn't just about creating a reasonable pace of life for your team; it's about producing better results and increased value for the organization by allowing people to more fully pour themselves into the work they're doing. Make sure to tie back the results to your strategy so that they understand why it's important to respect buffers; they may even begin to implement the strategy with their own teams.

Learn to say no so that your team can say yes, and build buffers around your team's activity. They will repay you with deeper engagement and better ideas. This will mean that they'll have more emotional bandwidth to deal with the complexities of creative collaboration and difficult clients. Better than that, they will feel more invested in the work and will be more likely to deliver breakthrough performance when it counts most.

CHECKPOINT

"White space" can sound like a negative thing to many organizations. After all, most organizations aspire to maximize the efficiency of its workers. However, efficiency isn't your goal. You're aiming for brilliance! Here are a few questions and exercises to help you protect your team's margin.

Actions

—Stop copying unnecessary people on e-mails. (Please.)

—Stop inviting nonessential people to meetings, or at least have a conversation with them about whether they need to be there.

—Cancel a recurring meeting. If necessary, add it back to the calendar, but not until you need it.

—Establish no-fly zone time for your team to do focused work.

Conversations

Have a conversation with key team members about the following:

—Do you feel like you have the margin you need to do your best work? How can I help?

—Where are you most overwhelmed right now, and what would give you reprieve?

—If you could make anything go away right now, what would it be and why?

Rituals

These rituals are also collected at the end of the book under weekly, monthly, and quarterly categories so that you can engage in them regularly.

Weekly: Look at your upcoming calendar and shift the schedule so that your team has blocks of time for focused work.

Monthly: Eliminate something from the calendar or tasks list this month so that your team has more time and attention for its most valuable projects.

Quarterly: Review your team's meeting schedule and organizational commitments—prune aggressively.

CHAPTER 10

BE THE MUSE

How to Spark Ideas

Ideas are like rabbits. You get a couple and learn how to handle them, and pretty soon you have a dozen.

—John Steinbeck

PRINCIPLE: To challenge your team members, push them outside their comfort zone.

If you, like me, have ever attempted to fly a drone and accidentally steered it directly into the single tree within a hundred yards of where you were standing, consider this humbling fact: a group of humans have remotely landed a vehicle on the surface of another planet.

Fifty years ago, the notion of landing a manmade vehicle on the surface of Mars was the stuff of science fiction. In fact, regardless of the optimism that permeated much of the scientific community during the early decades of the space race, the exploration of other planets seemed impossible. However, on August 6, 2012, the world watched as a team of scientists and engineers from NASA's Jet Propulsion Laboratory accomplished the unthinkable by landing the *Curiosity* rover safely on the surface of the red planet. The key to the successful landing was an ingenious new technology, developed by the JPL team, called Sky Crane. Because the rover was too heavy for traditional landing methods, the team had to instead go off script and invent a landing device that used engines on an outboard craft to slow the descent of the rover to the surface. It was a method that had never been used before and was considered by some to be too risky.

Adam Steltzner, who oversaw the development and deployment of the EDL (entry, descent, landing) phase of *Curiosity*, said that it was the very willingness of the team to entertain nontraditional ideas that allowed them to come up with the innovative landing technique. In his book *The Right Kind of Crazy*, he wrote, "The key to searching for the truth is to hold passionately to your beliefs while simultaneously not feeling entrenched in your position. . . . It's about letting ideas win, not people. It's about finding what's right, not being right."

The environment that you create for your team is critical to its ability to generate great ideas under pressure and even more critical to ensuring that the best ideas win. Commit to fostering an environment in which team members can share ideas freely, question assumptions, and play with new methods without fear of reprimand. Steltzner told me in an interview that one of the reasons that many teams get stuck in a rut is that they fear what he calls "the dark room," which means that they fear being in a place of uncertainty more than they fear failure. Many people would rather stay in a comfortable place and come up with a lot of mediocre ideas than risk venturing out of familiar territory in order to possibly generate a few brilliant ones. He offered this strong exhortation to creative teams: "Don't anticipate and die a death by worrying about that death. . . . Keep thinking, change your perspective, and don't stress."

No matter how uncomfortable or risky it feels, it's your job to keep your team in the dark room as long as necessary to have a breakthrough. Lock the door and confiscate their flashlights. Through good and bad, comfortable and uncomfortable, manage the idea-generation process from inspiration to execution. This requires (a) resourced inspiration and regularly planted seeds for your team, (b) effective flow of ideas, and (c) management of both the unfettered optimists and the sour pessimists before they derail your team's progress.

ABOUT BAD IDEAS . . .

Can we please—once and for all—dropkick to the curb the old cliché "There's no such thing as a bad idea"? Of course there is. There are terrible ideas. Awful, rotten, destructive, and irresponsible ideas. I've had a lot of them, and I'm sure you have too. When someone mutters this cliché in a meeting, they are trying to make everyone feel better about their bad ideas, but their words ring hollow. Everyone already knows the truth. (And the truth is, that last idea was a real stinker.)

At the same time, we need to loosen the filters that keep us from sharing those ideas. If you wait until every idea is fully formed before introducing it, you may miss a spark that lights someone else's fire. That's why even bad ideas can be valuable. Bad ideas are often the harbinger of good ones trying to break through. However, what you want are *qualified* bad ideas. They are not bad because they are completely irrelevant and a waste of everyone's time, but because they don't fully solve the problem. Still, they have useful parts.

On the flip side of the spectrum, great ideas often take time to develop and require more than the traditional brainstorming treatment used by many teams.

BREAKING UP IS HARD TO DO

Is there anything that elicits more eye rolls than the typical corporate brainstorm? You have actual *work* to do, and now you're called into a room to spitball ideas and try to come up with a breakthrough and do it in, oh, about forty-five minutes. Worse, a handful of people typically monopolize the conversation, and you end up checking your e-mail or half listening, waiting for permission to get back to the work that's piling up in your absence.

In the end, you rush to choose an idea, one that few people are excited about, and one that you know you'll probably be called back into a meeting to refine later.

Yes, there is unquestionable value in getting everyone together to leverage their shared perspectives and attack a problem. No doubt. However, there is a much more elegant and effective way to go about it. The best ideas are likely to come from a combination of individual *and* collective idea generation.

If you wait until every idea is fully formed before introducing it, you may miss a spark that lights someone else's fire.

First, assign homework. Several days before the meeting, make sure the team knows the specific problem that you're attacking during the idea session. (If you've already started to discuss meeting agendas and assign homework in advance, based upon the previous chapter on margin, you're ahead of the game.) Define the actual problem the team is solving, not just the project. The homework: come with three ideas for solving that problem. This will ensure that (a) they don't come into the meeting cold, and (b) you'll have some things to discuss from the very start instead of desperately trying to get everyone up to speed.

Many people—introverts and extroverts alike—do their best creative thinking on their own rather than in the midst of a group. By giving people a problem to work on in solo fashion, you empower them to explore it from their own perspective without the social, time, and political pressures that are baked into a team meeting. You also allow those who are naturally intimidated by speaking in group settings to distill their idea into shareable form before presenting it publicly. (Introverts unite!)

Second, begin the meeting by restating the problem and the objective, as well as the time frame for the idea session. Make certain people know that there is a definitive stop time so that they can give you their full attention and effort. Sitting in a poorly defined meeting is like drifting at sea, desperately scanning for land. Make sure everyone understands exactly what you're there to do and how you'll know you're finished.

Next, ask people to choose an idea they think has promise, that they came up with on their own, and to share it with the group. Go around the group and allow people to share one at a time until everyone has had an opportunity. Then open up to group discussion.

Which idea resonates the most with you?

Did anything you heard spark an insight or additional idea?

How did the ideas that were shared change your perception of the problem?

Does anyone have an additional idea—from the homework—that you think everyone should hear?

It's likely that a few of the ideas will initially gain the most traction within the group. Do not allow the most strong-willed person to dominate the conversation. You may also want to do multiple rounds of sharing if there is a lot of energy for the project. Make certain that everyone has an opportunity to share their ideas and insights. Nathan Hendricks from the brand design agency LPK once told me, "There are both fast and slow twitch people. Fast twitch people might throw out a bunch of junk in a meeting, but a lot of it is pretty bad. Slow twitch people are often less prolific when on the spot, but are best equipped to deal with the mess of a brainstorm meeting. So it's important not to discount people just because they aren't prolific in the moment. Try to find ways to include them in the meeting. They are often best at spotting the patterns." Talk to these "slow twitch" people ahead of the meeting, and ask them to be looking for any dots they think need to be connected or any strong ideas that are being overlooked. Give them a specific problem you'd like for them to focus on during the meeting to help them better spot patterns.

Finally, choose the leading idea(s) and determine next steps. Who will be accountable for developing it further? When will the group meet again to discuss progress? Leave an idea session with a clear understanding of next steps and specific accountability for them.

Much of the above seems like common sense—and it *is*—and yet once again, many leaders don't practice it. Instead, they rely on hastily called idea-generation sessions to try to solve problems, which means that some of the quieter and slower-processing team members won't have the opportunity to bring their best ideas to the table. The collective genius of the team will not be fully utilized. Allow team members the freedom to work in the way they are naturally wired. For some, that will mean shooting from the hip, but for others it will mean taking the time to mull over the problem over hours or days on their own before sharing their insights with the world.

Note: just structuring your idea sessions well is not sufficient to ensure that your team consistently produces great insights. You also need to do your part to resource their inspiration and ensure that your team is thinking systemically about the work. You must be a spark plug that ignites their creative fire.

PLANT SEEDS BEFORE YOU HARVEST

Let's say that you're a really undisciplined farmer, and you wake up one pretty spring day to find your neighbors out in their fields planting crops. However, you have a lot to do in the barn and around the house, and you really don't like planting, so you decide to put it off as long as possible. Every day you seem to find a new reason not to plant your crops, and because you're getting a lot of urgent things done around the farm, you even start to forget them altogether. Now let's say that it's several months later, and you notice your neighbors' crops are almost fully grown and ready for harvest, but you haven't even planted yet. You suddenly realize that no matter how hard you work to make up for your lack of discipline, you will never be able to plant seeds in time for a harvest this season. There are some things that simply cannot be rushed, because they take time to develop. You have missed your chance. You may have the cleanest barn, the sharpest tools, and the most-well-kept farmhouse, but without crops the farm produces no value.

If you neglect the most important things, then everything else ceases to matter. If you want to reap a harvest later, you have to plant seeds now. This requires consistently resourcing your team with inspiration to produce the best work down the line. Here are a few methods that work well for many leaders.

Feed the team's stimulus queue. Do you regularly funnel great resources to your team, like books, articles, or other kinds of inspiring stimuli, that might spark creative insights? All of these resources become fuel for future creative work.

Chris Andruss, a creative director, told me that the most important ritual in his life as it relates to his leadership is "overindexing" on information so that he is able to filter and pass on the most valuable information to the team. He reads magazines and books, listens to podcasts, and stays up on trends, all the while scanning for inspiring stimuli he can share with the people on his team who are doing the work. By curating and immersing his team in what is personally inspiring him, he is able to provide them with ideas and bits of inspiration they would never have come across otherwise.

If you want to lead your team's thinking and open them up to your vision, the best way to do it is to expose them to others who are doing similar things in a parallel field. Find stories in trade magazines or listen to podcast interviews with people who have solved a similar problem to the one that your team is working on. Any time you find a story of someone who took a unique approach to her work, share it with the team. You never know how and when it might spark the next big thing. Often, the best ideas for your industry will come from completely unrelated and unexpected places, and you'll only discover their relevance when you intentionally seek them out. By keeping these kinds of ideas and resources in front of your team on a regular basis, whether that means sharing and discussing them in a meeting or linking to them by e-mail and asking everyone to consider them, you're increasing the chances of an unexpected creative breakthrough. However, be careful not to overwhelm your team with stimuli. If you are constantly sending more stimuli than they can possibly (and responsibly) process, it will overwhelm them, or they will stop paying attention altogether. Maybe one or two great bits of stimuli a week are sufficient. (Don't be that crazy uncle who forwards every funny cat video or conspiracy theory he comes across.)

If you want to reap a harvest later, you have to plant seeds now.

Create a library full of stimuli. One company that I worked with created a central library for the organization. It was stocked with great books on leadership, management, and organizational life, as well as resources (and toys) that could spark new thinking and inspire unique conversations. It sat in the central common area of the workspace, and anyone in the organization could check out a resource whenever they needed a little extra spark. Additionally, if someone read a book that he thought would be of value to the team, he could donate it to the library so that others could benefit from it.

Consider the best books, magazines, and resources that you've experienced along the way, and dedicate a budget to resourcing a central library for your team. Additionally, consider encouraging people to highlight or underline things that they find valuable and add notes in the margins (with their initials and a date) so that others can see how the book is affecting their thinking. By encouraging this, you're facilitating an asynchronous meeting of the minds.

Create a virtual stimulus queue. In addition to the physical library, consider creating a space where people can post interesting things they come across, ideas they have, or other potentially useful inspiring bits of stimuli. Even better, make it a place where the archive of inspiring items can be perused for future inspiration and where team members can comment on ideas and stimuli. None of what is shared has to relate to something you're currently working on. Instead, it's simply a well to draw from when your team is looking for a new idea or seeking a spark of inspiration on a difficult problem.

Do your best to cultivate an environment in which sharing inspiration is the expectation of everyone on the team, and the continual attempts to mash up potentially useful ideas is celebrated. More than anything, make sure that you are modeling the behavior that you want from your team. Share freely, connect openly, and discuss frequently.

CREATE HUNTING TRAILS

Chris Michel is an entrepreneur who has built and sold multiple businesses, including Affinity Labs and Military.com. He has spent a lot of time both as an entrepreneur and an investor among the ranks of company founders and start-up participants and has a unique perch from which to follow companies from idea to rollout.

"One kind of entrepreneur says 'I really want to be an entrepreneur, and I want to start a company badly,'" he told me. "They are simply going around the room picking ideas out of the blue. However, the effective kind of entrepreneur is already an expert in something, or is passionate about a topic, and is able to spot pain points and develop a solution."

Many people think that the best ideas are "out there," somewhere.

However, the best ideas often emerge by paying attention to our pain points and by making connections between seemingly disparate ideas that are already right under our noses.

In our previous home, the window of my home office looked out onto a green belt, so I would see interesting wildlife, ranging from deer and coyotes to hawks and turkey vultures, on a regular basis. Another frequent visitor was a neighborhood cat our kids had named Bella, though we didn't know her actual name. We weren't certain where Bella lived, but she was a near constant presence around our home.

As I sat staring out the window, contemplating my next sentence, I would occasionally see Bella make an appearance behind our house. She always paced slowly to the edge of the woods, then carefully along the edge of the woods, and back down the side where there's a wild grass area. Next, she'd slowly stalk along the back of our storage shed, around the side, and make a beeline to the back of our house. Finally, she'd walk all around our deck and the bushes, then take off. This happened two to three times each day. I called it her "hunting trail."

I assure you that Bella was not hurting for food. She caught lots and lots and lots of prey. I'd witnessed it a few times, and she was tenacious. When she was walking the trail, she was intense. She was looking for prey, and she was very opportunistic.

> Many people think that the best ideas are "out there," somewhere. However, the best ideas often emerge by paying attention to our pain points and by making connections between seemingly disparate ideas that are already right under our noses.

She followed the same routine every day—and at multiple times that probably correlated to when her prey was most active. She was looking instinctually for a break in the norm as she went about this routine, such as a scurrying creature in the grass, and when she saw that disruption, she pounced. She knew how to put herself in the right place at the right time to have the best chance for taking advantage of those opportunities.

I think there is a lot to learn from Bella. Just like her, we need hunting trails, or routines and practices in our daily life that put us in a position where we're likely to experience creative insights or breakthroughs. Many people don't have hunting trails. Instead, they are like a cat wandering aimlessly through the neighborhood waiting for a mouse or bird to wander across its path.

Brilliant breakthroughs are usually the result of structured exploration, not random wandering. Here are a few hunting trails that you can use with your team to help you generate ideas and insights.

What are we assuming to be true, or false? Challenge your team to regularly question assumptions about your customer, your industry, and your competitors. It's so easy to slip into ruts of thought simply because you are living with assumptions about what is and isn't possible. Identify these assumptions, and play with alternatives by asking "What might we do if this wasn't true (or false)?" For example, are you making assumptions about who your customers are and what they want? The best way to get it to them? Maybe or maybe not, but it's a question you should ask frequently. In addition, follow it up with this thought exercise: *If something was a false assumption, how would we approach it differently? What might we try that no one else is currently even considering because they are following the same assumption?*

This is a powerful hunting trail because, although it may not result in a breakthrough every time, the ones that do turn up are likely to be valuable because your competitors are probably overlooking them as well.

Where have we seen something like this before? A key reason why people get stuck is their inability to learn from the experiences of others. Push your team to seek inspiration outside of your industry. Who else has solved a problem similar to the one that you are currently trying to solve, and how did they do it? What lessons might you be able to apply to your own situation in order to achieve breakthrough? Share the story of someone who is revolutionizing her industry, and discuss how you might apply her method to your own work. Talk about a trend that's currently catching fire in another industry, and ask how it might apply to a project you're working on.

Challenge your team members to ask "How might this thing I'm experiencing apply to the work I'm doing?" as they are reading, talking with a peer, or even watching television.

When you are leading a team idea session, and you reach an impasse, ask the team to consider: "What about this problem seems familiar to you?" Alternatively, challenge team members to bring one example of something "out there" that they think is relevant to the current problem you are solving.

What if we had no constraints? Or what if we were completely restrained? It's easy to slip into rote behavior because of a feeling of being constrained by resources, time, or attention. What would you do if you had no constraints? How would it change your approach to the problem? What kinds of solutions might you offer? While this might seem like a pie in the sky exercise, it's far from it. It challenges you to shed any excess baggage you are carrying around and consider the purest form of action, unencumbered by resource limitations. For example, "If we had all the money in the world, how would we do this project?" Push your team to consider completely "blue sky" ideas that seem thoroughly impractical and very unlikely to be executed. It costs you little to play this game. Thoughts are cheap, but missing a potentially valuable idea because you were artificially constrained can be tremendously costly.

Or "If we had no resources to throw at this, how would we solve this problem?" How would it change our approach? What might we have to try? How would we innovate our methods? You may discover a completely new avenue of exploration results from taking away resource crutches.

What will success look like in one year (or five)? Challenge your team to consider what a solved problem actually looks like for your customer or for the organization. If someone were to write a newspaper article about what your team has accomplished, what would it say? Begin with what it will look like for you to have created a product, system, or solution for your customer, and how life for the customer will be different as a result. Often this thought exercise will open up new ways of thinking about the problem and push your team to generate ideas from a position of empathy for the end customer rather than from a desire to push through the project.

DO A STIMULUS DIVE

Getting outside the confines of your normal workspace can help your team think in fresh ways about the problem you're trying to solve and help them gain better focus. If you're working on an especially challenging project or problem and seem to be at an impasse, plan an outing for your team to help spark new thinking.

I led one team, complete with instant cameras, on a photography expedition around the neighborhood, with the challenge to snap images that could spark a new way of thinking about a client's key products. By getting out of their normal routine and methods and thinking more visually, team members came away with a brand message that greatly clarified their offering. Another team went to a baseball game to rethink a client project, and it helped completely reframe the problem as a customer experience, which was not how they were previously considering it. Another team did a dumpster dive (actually just in the alleys, not the actual dumpsters) in New York City to try to find "treasures" that would spark inspiration for their brand. They came away a little more smelly, but with a new perspective on how tiny, discarded treasures represent an intimate portrait of a season in someone's life, and it gave them a fresh perspective on how to connect with customers. All of these are examples of a "stimulus dive" or an intentional outing that's meant to push you outside your comfort zone and thought ruts.

Here's how to plan one for your team:

1. Identify and define the specific problem that you're trying to solve. This isn't a field trip; it's a working session. You are trying to use the stimulus from a new environment to open you to new ideas. Make certain that the team knows the desired outcome of the stimulus dive and the specific problem that you're trying to solve. If you go into the stimulus dive with a lack of focus, it will probably be a waste of time.

2. Instruct your team to observe, then apply. The goal is to take note of the environment and use what you experience to try to solve the problem. A solution isn't going to appear in its entirety,

fully formed, but something that you see could spark a thought, which then sparks another, and soon you have a potential idea forming.

The goal is to use seemingly disconnected bits of stimuli to open new paths of thinking, so it's going to take some effort. Encourage your team to ask, "How does this apply to the problem?" and to keep working until it experiences a breakthrough.

3. Work in pairs. Although there can be some value in working alone, and some of the introverts on your team may actually prefer that, there is much more value in working in pairs or small teams so that you can leverage the perspective of the other person. It also creates baked-in accountability for everyone to stay on task.

4. Separate, then come back together and talk about what you saw. Send your team out to observe and apply on their own, then come back together and talk about what happened. Each pair should get a chance to share their thoughts with the team; then the team should discuss the ideas and build on them.

This is one of those exercises that can feel a little risky for a leader. After all, it's a lot of time (and resources) that could result in nothing, so it would be tempting to shy away from it. In addition, your organization may frown upon these kinds of seemingly frivolous activities. I encourage you to find relatively low-risk ways of experimenting with a stimulus dive before booking an entire day and renting out a venue for the team. Once you've been able to prove the effectiveness of the method, you can make a case for taking progressively larger steps toward pushing your team out of its comfort zone.

MANAGE THE SPARK AND THE SCORPION

Have you ever met people who like every single idea they hear? They are so optimistic that they believe they can make anything work out for the best. They are constantly bouncing off the walls with energy and tossing out radical new ideas and ways of approaching a problem. They are idea machines.

And, unfortunately, they are massively disruptive to your team dynamic.

What! Don't you *want* your team to generate lots of ideas?

Of course you do. However, there is a difference between generating a lot of ideas at the appropriate point in the process and lacking discernment for when it's time to shut the idea machine down. You cannot continue to generate ideas forever, or you will never execute on any of them.

I call these perpetual idea machines sparks, because they are constantly offering up "What if . . ." and "Hey, let's try . . ." kinds of ideas, even when conversations have been closed. Although they inject a certain amount of energy into the group, they also distract from the real task at hand, which is executing the decisions that the team has already made.

On the other hand, there are people who have never met an idea they liked. They find the fault in everything, even before it's been given a fair chance. "Yeah, but . . ." is their favorite phrase. I call these people scorpions because they like to sting and kill anything that's unfamiliar or has the potential to be disruptive. Needless to say, scorpions can be deadly to your team dynamic. They can quickly shut down idea generation before your team gains traction or prevent some of the more hesitant people on your team from sharing their burgeoning ideas.

In order to keep your team inspired, you have to manage the spark and the scorpion effectively.

The Spark: You don't want to pour water on the spark's creative fire, but you also don't want to let it get out of control and consume the entire forest. The best way to manage the spark is to create clear expectations about when and where new ideas are welcome; when the steel door has shut, new ideas are no longer needed (or helpful).

1. Constantly reiterate the stage that you're in with a project and the kinds of ideas that will be helpful at the moment. The best way to channel the spark's energy is to focus it in ways that will be genuinely useful. Give sparks specific problems to tackle. For example, find an upcoming problem that you don't want everyone thinking about yet and let sparks get a head start on it. Give them permission and space to think as wildly as they'd like and to get all of their ideas out on the table. Also, use their energy strategically at certain stages of the project to inject fresh thinking. For example, if the team hits an impasse on a project they're not involved in, invite them into the conversation to get a lot of new thinking into the mix.

2. Invite ideas, but ask that they be an ongoing dialogue between the two of you and not with the entire team. The most destructive aspect of the spark's perpetual creative engine is

the distraction it creates. Give them an outlet for their ideas, but limit their destructive and distracting potential by acting as a filter.

3. Have an honest conversation about when and where you need their creative energy. Don't be afraid to ask them to temper their creative input on certain projects—those that are past idea phase—and to channel it instead into others that need a spark. However, make sure that they understand that you value their energy and passion for ideas when they are time appropriate. You don't want them throttling their engine, but you also can't have them lapping the team over and over when it's simply distracting to the process.

The Scorpion: Scorpions are a little easier to manage because their effect on the team is quite obvious and immediate. There's nothing that douses the team's energy more than someone who immediately discounts every idea they hear.

1. Articulate the expectations at the beginning of every meeting, and reinforce to the team that you're thinking about possibilities now, not practicalities. There will be a time to critique, but not in the moment when ideas are shared.

2. Ask the scorpions to share the first idea in your meeting so that they are immediately invested in the outcome. Rather than sitting back and critiquing ideas indiscriminately, you're making them exhibit vulnerability from the start and increasing the likelihood that they will feel invested in the conversation.

3. If they get out of hand in a meeting, but not unreasonably so, pull them aside afterward and reinforce your expectations. Tell them that you value their critical thinking, and recognize how important it is in the big picture, but that you'd like for them to temper their criticism during the idea sessions until it's asked for. Do it in a light and casual way, though. Again, you don't want to make them self-conscious. You simply want them to use their critical superpowers for good and not evil.

Stay ahead of your team, resource their inspiration, and push them outside their comfort zone. Then, make sure that you are clearly defining the problems you're trying to solve, and be very clear about which ideas do and don't hit the mark. Over many months, you'll begin to see your team's creative ideas improve in both quantity and quality, and you may even learn to love to brainstorm again.

CHECKPOINT

Your team cannot produce brilliant work without great ideas. It's your job to provide the creative spark they need and to foster the environment in which ideas can grow. Here are a few questions and exercises that you can build into your rhythm to help you keep your team inspired:

Actions

—Start a stimulus queue (or library) for your team. Ask team members to bring in (or recommend) books or resources that everyone should experience.

—Plan a stimulus dive to get your team outside of its normal surroundings. Choose a problem to solve, take your team to an off-site location, and use your surroundings to help everyone think differently about the problem.

Conversations

Have a conversation with key team members about the following:

—In general, do you like coming up with ideas on your own or in a group format? Why?

—How inspired are you right now by the work?

—What's the greatest thing you've read or seen lately, and how is it affecting your perspective?

—What was the last idea you had that excited you, and why?

Rituals

These rituals are also collected at the end of the book under weekly, monthly, and quarterly categories so that you can engage in them regularly.

Weekly: Send an e-mail with a key resource or article to your team and explain why you're sending it. Make sure it's something that will inspire team members to think in new ways about the work or open their minds to new possibilities.

Monthly: Consider what resources you can add to your team's stimulus library to help it stay inspired. What have you read or watched recently that you wish more of your team had access to?

Quarterly: Plan a stimulus dive for your team around a big project. Choose a project with a long horizon (not one that's due next week) and plan a team outing. Make sure that you go into the stimulus dive with a specific, focused problem and that the location will provide ample inspiration for the team. (No coffee shops or shopping malls, please. Get people out of their routine.)

CHAPTER 11

FIGHT WELL

How to Manage Conflict

There is nothing so annoying as to have two people go right on talking while you're interrupting.

—Mark Twain

PRINCIPLE: To create stability, recognize that conflict isn't a bad thing. In fact, it's a sign of a healthy and productive team.

If you crave emotional comfort, you probably need to find a new line of work. Leading creative work is the least emotionally safe role you'll find. It's never easy to speak truth to someone and burst his overinflated ego. It's always challenging and uncomfortable to tell someone that she doesn't have the skills to finish a job, even though she is the nicest person in the office. It breaks your heart to have to fire someone even though you know that he has a family at home depending on his income. All of these actions are terribly uncomfortable, even when they are necessary and right.

You never, *ever* want to have to do any of the above. So, in the moment, it's easy to revert to whatever is emotionally safe and ignore major performance or attitude issues on your team. That is a slippery slope that leads to confused expectations and a lack of trust and respect. If your team sees you taking the comfortable route instead of doing what's right, it won't trust your objectivity. And it won't respect any boundaries that you set because your expectations are subject to change with your emotions.

People who crave emotional comfort avoid conflict at all costs. However, if there is no conflict on your team it likely means that (a) everyone is "phoning it in" and they aren't really bringing their unique perspective to the table or (b) accountability is spread so thin on your team that no one feels fully invested in the outcome, so people don't care what happens. Either of these two options is a sign of disengagement and decline.

This is also why I shudder when I hear a leader refer to a team or the company culture as "family." No, no, no. You are *not* family. Families are connected by blood or by bonds that can't be broken, and membership in a family is unconditional. However, membership in your organization requires adoption of a certain set of behaviors and subscription to cultural ideals and norms. If at any point someone violates those norms, his connection to your team is subject to termination. It is misleading and maybe even a little manipulative to your team members to give them the impression that they are a part of something like a family. It is often insecurity on the part of a leader that leads to such sentiments.

Although conflict is normal, you shouldn't go seeking it. However, if you've hired properly, it means that you will have a lot of talented people with diverse points of view on your team. This also means that these highly creative people are likely to disagree about the best direction for the work and will have valid reasons for their beliefs. Your job is to encourage dissent and provide an environment in which people can speak their mind, but also to rally everyone around the idea that is best for your stakeholders.

FIGHTING FAIR

I was once quizzing a manager about some of the collaborative dynamics of his team. I asked about hiring and collaboration, and when we got around to the topic of how the team handles conflict, he replied, "Oh, we're about the healthiest team you'll ever encounter. We never fight."

"Never?!" I asked, barely holding back my surprise.

"Never! I can't remember the last time we had a significant argument."

Though I had enough presence of mind in the moment to hold my tongue, every part of me wanted to scream, "Healthy?! Healthy?! You're the most dysfunctional team I've ever encountered!" In fact, that was the truth. There was so much conflict bubbling up on the team that it was impossible to hide, but because there was never a forum to address it, the conflict was showing up in less visible but more subversive ways, such as private hallway conversations or passive-aggressive, snarky comments in e-mails.

Your team is not a family. Don't treat it like one.

Healthy teams fight. Some managers don't want to accept this principle, because they want everything to be easy and smooth. In truth, without open conflict on the team, you are the fast track to mediocrity. However, there is an important caveat to this principle: healthy teams fight *fair*. They have clear rules around how they will handle conflict, and they follow those rules in the interest of both the work and one another.

Great leaders embrace healthy conflict and use it to sharpen the team, whereas poor leaders try to prematurely resolve it.

RULES FOR FIGHTING FAIR

It's vital to ensure that everyone is on the same page about the rules for conflict before things get heated. Once you're in the throes of an argument, it's difficult to ease up on the gas pedal, and it's highly likely that something will happen that could permanently damage the team dynamic. It only takes one errant comment or one blatant disregard of a person's feelings to result in days or weeks of repair efforts. Therefore, strive to remind your team of the rules of fair fighting on a regular basis so that no one is caught off guard. Also, make sure that there are consequences when someone breaks one of the rules. If you say you're going to fight fair as a team, but nothing happens when someone steps over the line, you risk losing credibility with the team and—again—damaging the team dynamic.

1. Fight over *Ideas*, Not over Personality

If you've done a good job of hiring, then you should have a wide-ranging and diverse set of ideas floating around about which direction to take with a project. Many of those ideas are going to be in conflict with one another, so allow the team to mix it up and go to bat for their favorite. However, it's also important that you not allow conflict over ideas and direction to become personal. Personal conflict can be the death of a team, and it's your job as the leader to ensure that everyone is fighting for *something*, not against *someone*.

Great leaders embrace healthy conflict and use it to sharpen the team, whereas poor leaders try to prematurely resolve it.

For example, "That's a dangerous idea, because it ignores a key piece of data" is different from "You're always ignoring important facts, and your idea is dangerous." Both statements are expressing the same concept, but one is a statement about the merits of the idea, and the other is making a statement about the competence of the individual.

When sides or cults of personality emerge within an organization, it will destroy the team dynamic. Make certain that your team is fighting for ideas, not choosing sides.

2. Find the Merits; Don't Just Destroy

As we discussed in an earlier chapter, there are *terrible* ideas. There are ideas that make you question the sanity of the person introducing them. ("*Really*, Joe? That's the best you've got?") However, the quality of the ideas matters less to your long-term team dynamic than what you do with them when they arise. You don't have to celebrate bad ideas, but you do have to have some rules about how they are handled so that you don't squash the team's morale.

We've all been a part of meetings in which one team member is firing torpedoes at every new idea without offering anything constructive to the conversation. This seriously disrupts the team's mojo and ultimately undermines the effort to get to a great result. You cannot tolerate this behavior. Require that everyone contribute, not simply destroy.

However, it's often clear to everyone that an idea isn't right even though a better one hasn't yet appeared. In these cases, it is impossible to replace the idea with a better one. Instead, you should encourage the team to find the merits in the idea before completely dismissing it.

"I don't think it will work, but I like _____."

"This reminds me of the time when we _____, and it worked out well."

"What if we took just one part of the idea and used it to _____."

When the team takes this approach, it (a) validates the parts of the idea that could be constructive and (b) simultaneously makes it clear that the idea needs to be put out to pasture. You are also able to have a collective conversation about why the idea doesn't work rather than just dismissing it, which serves to clarify the team's overall vision for the project.

3. Agree on Your Common Objectives from the Start

From the very beginning of an argument, the entire team should agree that the ultimate success of the project trumps everyone's personal stake. Team members must commit to get behind whichever idea comes out on top, even if it's not their own. Otherwise, team members may hold grudges over time, engage in political games, and begin to form alliances with other team members to ensure that their own ideas come out on top.

Whenever you sense that a public disagreement is coming on, remind your team of its blanket commitment to the objectives and that all voices will be considered in the conversation before a final decision is reached. However, no matter which direction you go, someone is going to be unhappy. That's simply the nature of creative work. Thus, it's important that the team sees the project not as an individual win-or-lose venture, but as a collective one.

All of this *sounds* much easier than it actually is. When you're in the heat of the moment, mixing egos, ideas, identities, and politics, the conversation can get truly ugly. That's why it's so critical to establish the ground rules during times of peace so that you're not trying to implement them during the fog of war.

LEAD WITH COMPASSION

One reason why conflict seeps in and overtakes a team is the inability to see things through the eyes of others.

Recently, I was flying to Telluride, Colorado, for a speaking engagement and found out upon arriving at the airport that my flight was delayed. This was a major problem, because I had a very tight turnaround in Denver, and I feared that any delay whatsoever would prevent me from being able to make my connecting flight—the last of the day and the only one that could get me to my event on time. Needless to say, I was very frustrated. Once I discovered that the delay was due to a flight attendant scheduling error, I was livid.

As I sat there fuming, my attention was drawn across the tarmac to another airplane. I saw some kind of commotion, with a dozen or more airline employees and a few parked automobiles all gathered around the rear end of a large plane. Then, a long, black car with twin U.S. flags on the hood turned a corner, drove slowly down the tarmac, and parked directly behind the airplane. I saw a young, blond woman wearing a black dress exit the car, and she was greeted by a man in a suit who put his arm around her and escorted her to the side of the plane. I wondered what was going on. Was this a diplomat returning to Washington, D.C.? A member of Congress? A celebrity in town to film a movie receiving a celebratory send-off? What if *this* has something to do with my delay!

Then my heart sank.

Out of the cargo hold of the plane, six airline employees pulled a casket draped in a U.S. flag—a soldier who'd been killed in battle was arriving home to be buried by his family. Even across the tarmac, I could see the woman's legs give way when she saw the wooden box. It was almost as if reality and finality hit all at once in that moment. She collapsed into the arms of the suited man. Then she reached out and placed one hand on the casket and kept it there for what seemed to me like minutes, though it was only a few seconds.

The casket was loaded into the back of a hearse, and the entire motorcade circled around, followed a reverse path back down the tarmac and around the corner and out of sight. I watched the remaining airline employees as they hugged one another for comfort, and one at a time they ambled back to their regular jobs.

The entire event took only a few moments, but it absolutely turned my world upside down. Any flight delay seemed so insignificant. I felt petty. Frankly, I was ashamed. I was worried about having to run across the airport to catch my connection while someone's world was falling apart only a few yards away.

Perspective is everything in life and in leadership. Experiencing the suffering of someone else, even from a distance, reminded me that behind every decision, system, success, and failure is a human being trying to succeed. I suddenly realized that no one had planned to delay my flight, and no one had planned in advance to try to derail my trip. Behind the scenes were people doing their best. Yes, there needs to be accountability when things go wrong. Yes, it's unacceptable to consistently fail. However, you can hold compassion and accountability hand in hand. In fact, you must.

The word *compassion* comes from Latin roots that mean "with" and "to suffer." When you show compassion, you enter into the suffering of another person, and you choose to see the world from their perspective. Again, this doesn't mean that you accept or endorse their failures, or that they shouldn't feel the repercussions of them, but that your discipline is coming from a place of understanding and mutual suffering.

You have no idea what's going on—*really* going on—in the lives of your team members. Everything could look great on the surface, but behind the scenes their relationships are frayed, their children are sick, or they are struggling with some other personal problem. When you fail to exhibit compassion, you might be layering stress onto their already overstressed lives.

You can hold compassion and accountability hand in hand. In fact, you must.

Here are a few principles to help you deal with conflict in a more compassionate way:

Never discipline reactively. You've probably heard urban legends about leaders firing people in an elevator or on the spot in a meeting for making a silly comment. Unless it's a matter of outright rebellion or disrespect and you need to set an example for the team, you should never discipline someone reactively. You never know what is going on in their world that influenced their behavior.

Instead of reactive discipline that you might regret later, strive to exhibit compassion. If the behavior was out of character, ask them why they felt the need to do it and what they think might have prompted it. If it's a new pattern, point it out to them and establish clear boundaries about what will happen if it continues.

Aim for empathy. To empathize means to feel along with someone else. Not to mentally assent to what the person must be feeling, but to take the time to really enter into the experience of the other person, to remind yourself of a time when you were in a similar situation, and to strive to feel what the person might be feeling at the moment. Before you make any major decision that will affect someone on your team, stop to consider how the decision will affect the person and make the compassionate choice, even if it's one the person won't like. (Compassion and compliance are not the same thing.)

Also, recognize that a job is just one part of a person's life. Yes, there must be accountability when someone makes a mistake or has a bad attitude, but sometimes that could be the result of unseen things happening in other areas of the person's life. When you strive to act with empathy, you can more clearly see how those dots might interconnect and be affecting the person's behavior, especially if it's out of character.

Act compassionately, even when it hurts. Sometimes the compassionate thing is to do what the other person least wants. We tend to confuse doing what's in the other person's best interest with doing the thing the person prefers. These are not always one and the same. You do often have more information, and you're able to see things from an elevated perspective.

One of the most compassionate things done to me early in my career was when someone removed me from a position of leadership because I'd developed blinders that were affecting my ability to lead my team. I was so certain that I was right about a restructuring effort that I simply couldn't see any other point of view, even when confronted with evidence that I was wrong. After going a few rounds in the ring with me, my manager pulled me from my direct oversight of the team and shifted me to a position where I could lead vision but had no hands-on management of personnel. It seemed so unfair in the moment, and almost prompted me to quit, but I soon came to realize that I was making it all about me and not about the ultimate outcome we were trying to achieve. Over the course of several months, I came to see my manager's decision as a great lesson in doing the right thing even when difficult. I was too much in my head and needed to be shaken out of it. It was compassion.

Although it might seem unfair or cruel in the moment to the other person, doing the compassionate thing might mean doing something painful in the short run that is beneficial in the long run. Some leaders act to protect themselves or their own feelings, or they capitulate in the face of pressure because it's emotionally convenient, and they'd rather not have to deal with the discomfort of stirring the pot. However, this only creates greater issues down the road. Acting with compassion means being willing to do the right thing, even when it's uncomfortable in the moment.

DON'T DRAW LINES IN THE SAND . . .

Sarah was a brilliant young leader at a large, fast-growing organization. Her team truly respected her abilities, and the team was generally performing great, but she had one fatal flaw: she always had to have the upper hand on everything. Whenever she perceived that someone was overreaching his or her authority or challenging her own, she felt the need to shove the person back into his or her proper place by asserting herself in often pointless ways, such as escalating a deadline or canceling a meeting, forcing everyone to shuffle their calendar to reschedule. This sometimes caused her team members to walk on eggshells around her or to simply wait until Sarah would tell them what to do, because they didn't want to have to deal with her last-minute expectations.

It's natural when you feel like your territory is being threatened to respond by drawing lines in the sand to assert your authority, but that is often nothing more than an insecure response to a perceived threat. When you start to feel like things are slipping out of control, you immediately assert yourself to show who's in charge, even when it really accomplishes little. Although healthy boundaries are necessary for the functioning of any team, arbitrary lines in the sand do nothing but complicate the relational dynamics of the team and put everyone on edge.

I hear you asking, "But who would be petty enough to draw arbitrary lines just to assert their authority?" Do you *really* need to ask? We do it all the time, reactively, when we feel threatened.

"OK, if you're going to do *that*, then I'm going to need *this*."

"If you're going to cancel *that* meeting, then I'm going to schedule *this* one."

"OK, we'll go with your idea, but I want it to also have *this* in it."

All of these are examples of reactive boundary setting. When you behave in this way, it forces others to make a choice in the moment to comply or fight, often needlessly and over nothing more than ego. Leaders who resort to reactive tactics often do so out of insecurity or a fear of losing control of the team.

What is your response when you feel that your authority is being challenged? Do you feel the need to lash out and assert yourself, or are you confident in your abilities? Consider a time when you've responded reactively to a threat. Why did you respond that way? Was it the result of insecurity? A personal grudge? Raw ego? How might you have handled the situation differently?

Now, how will you respond the next time you feel threatened? Instead of asserting yourself pointlessly, reconnect with your core values and the already established boundaries you've set for the team. Instead of forcing control, lean into influence.

. . . BUT DON'T LET PEOPLE STOMP ON YOUR SAND CASTLE

Now, having just spent a lot of time telling you not to play arbitrary power games, let me offer some counteradvice: don't let someone publicly disrespect you without consequence.

There is a big difference between respectful disagreement and disruptive behavior. You can't afford to let someone undercut your authority in front of the team without consequence, because you are tacitly granting permission to everyone else to do the same. It's one thing to allow healthy disagreement over ideas and direction—this is to be expected and celebrated. It's another thing altogether to allow that disagreement to devolve into accusation or downright disrespectful commentary on your leadership. Your team members must exercise the same standards of healthy conflict toward you that they exercise toward their peers.

Very few people have the guts to publicly berate their team leader, but it certainly happens. I've seen it on multiple occasions, and it gets ugly. Worse, it can cultivate a culture of disrespect that eventually results in infighting and contempt. Once this dynamic takes root, the team is like a jumbo jet in a tailspin—almost impossible to recover.

When someone publicly crosses the line, handle it directly and in the moment. You can't wait until later, because conflict that arises in the group needs to be handled in the group. Model for everyone that you're not going to tolerate this behavior toward you or other members of the team. Here are a few tips for doing so:

Pause to allow the person's words to sink in. Don't immediately jump to counter the comment, or you will trigger a combative situation. A strategic pause will force the person to consider his or her tone and may in and of itself deescalate the situation. There are times when silence is the most effective counterargument.

Ask the person to clarify the statement. Sometimes, in the heat of the moment, people say things that they don't mean. They get overly emotionally vested in an idea, they still feel the sting of being passed over for an opportunity a few months back, or somehow they associate you with that terrible high school track coach who was forever telling them how they would never measure up. People say stupid things, and they immediately regret them. Offer an olive branch rather than responding in anger. Remember: the leader gets to take the most arrows to the chest, whether you want to or not.

Reiterate the principle of respect for others. Make certain that everyone present knows that you aren't defending your own ego but instead are defending the very culture of the team. Also, don't allow others to jump to your defense, even though it feels good. You don't want to incite a war within the team. Use this as a learning example for the team about how to handle conflict when it arises. There are going to be hot tempers from time to time, and people will say stupid things, so you need to model how to deal with it in a nonegocentric way.

Have a follow-up conversation in private. Close the loop after the meeting so that there is absolutely no ambiguity about where your relationship with the offending team member stands. Never allow a temporary argument to turn into a cold war. It's terrible for the team, and it's an unnecessary complication to your ability to lead. Follow up immediately, discuss what happened, and put it behind you.

You must be secure enough as a leader to allow disagreement, but you cannot tolerate disrespect. The line can blur, but the more you tolerate behavior that you know to be destructive, the more blurry those lines become. Over time, you train your team that the only way to get its way is to "power up," which is the exact opposite of what you really want to reinforce.

CLEARING HONEYSUCKLE

Our home has a series of bushes that shield it from the street and allow us a degree of privacy. The bushes also bloom with the most beautiful, lavender-colored flowers in the summer. It's one of the things we love about where we live. I vaguely remember a conversation with our neighbor, a landscaper, shortly after we moved in, about minding the honeysuckle in the bushes so that it doesn't spread; however, being someone who isn't overly obsessed with lawn and garden care, I kind of shrugged it off at the time. In fact, I shrugged it off for a few years.

I wish I hadn't.

This summer, I discovered two things: first, the lavender flowers didn't bloom; second, the honeysuckle had not only spread, but it had completely overtaken the bushes. There was now more honeysuckle than bush, and when I lifted it to look underneath, I discovered that the canopy it created had prevented sunlight from reaching the bushes and had ultimately killed an entire row of them. I then spent a full afternoon

You must be secure enough as a leader to allow disagreement, but you cannot tolerate disrespect.

cutting the honeysuckle out at the root and removing it from the bushes. Unfortunately, I also had to cut out several dead bushes that had been suffocated by the invasive honeysuckle.

Most of the biggest problems we face as leaders don't begin that way. They seem like relatively harmless quirks or nuisances that aren't worth our time. However, minor problems left untended can grow into something more substantial and damaging. Then we not only have to correct the initial problem anyway, but we also have to deal with the additional destruction it has caused.

If I had created a twice-yearly rhythm of cutting off new honey-suckle growth, I would still have my bushes intact and my pretty flowers. Because it was inconvenient to deal with a small problem *now*, I wound up with a big problem *later*. In a similar way, it's a good idea for leaders to have a regular rhythm of sweeping for problems to identify them before they become a bigger issue. This doesn't mean calling team members in for an intensive conversation or calling out every single misalignment that arises, but it does mean dedicating time at regular intervals to look for issues where they aren't necessarily going to be apparent on the surface.

Dedicate time once per month to consider the following questions:

Am I seeing hints of misalignment within the team? Have you noticed off-target remarks or strange "out of left field" behavior that could indicate that there is a lack of clarity around what you are really trying to do? Are there any little areas of conflict that should be dealt with publicly, or at least among a small group of people, so that they don't grow into greater misalignment or organizational tension?

Is there any budding relational tension? Have you noticed any odd, off-the-cuff comments or sharp retorts that could indicate that there are personality problems brewing? Are there any personality conflicts that are in danger of threatening the team's focus? Try to notice and get ahead of these before someone makes a comment in a meeting that suddenly takes things to another level.

Are new resource constraints creating pressure or tension? Does your team have everything it needs to be able to do its job well, or are resources dwindling to an unhealthy level? This may not seem like a big deal at first, but over time frustration with limited money, time, or bandwidth can add up to a bigger revolt.

Is there any frustration with organizational direction? Sometimes decisions made by the powers that be can have unintended trickle-down consequences for your team. Have you noticed any budding conflict or complaining about something happening in your organization? It's best to get ahead of it before it becomes something more disruptive.

It's tempting to overlook all of the above, because they are emotionally uncomfortable conversations. However, when you ignore minor areas of conflict, you create space for them to grow, like ignoring a small brush fire because it has not yet consumed the entire forest. Address small conflicts as they arise, and you'll be less likely to experience major ones that derail your team.

No one likes conflict, but it is a necessary part of creative productivity. If we all agree, it probably means that we're settling for the safest answer, which means settling for mediocrity at best. Encourage dissent on your team, keeping it within the boundaries of healthy disagreement. Further, if you refuse to do the emotionally convenient thing, you will maintain the trust and respect of those you lead.

CHECKPOINT

As it is with much of leadership, you must do what's right even when it's uncomfortable. Here are a few ways to stay ahead of conflict so that it doesn't derail your team.

Actions

—Pick a fight. (OK, a healthy one.) Encourage someone to raise a dissent over an important project or issue.

—Share the principles of fair fighting with your team so that they know the ground rules before things get heated.

Conversations

Have a conversation with key team members about the following:

—Is there anything we're doing right now that you disagree with? Why?

—Are there any conflicts on our team that you think I'm unaware of?

—Is there anything I'm doing right now that's preventing you from speaking truth to me? How can I be more open?

Rituals

These rituals are also collected at the end of the book under weekly, monthly, and quarterly categories so that you can engage in them regularly.

Weekly: Take some time to consider the interactions on your team and note where there are any potential conflicts or signs of dissension.

Monthly: Have a conversation with each of your core team members about their level of satisfaction with the work and the team's overall dynamics.

Quarterly: Reiterate your team's core principles and review the rules of fair fighting.

CHAPTER 12

BE A LEADER
WORTH FOLLOWING

Becoming a leader is synonymous with becoming yourself. It is precisely that simple and it is also that difficult.

—Warren Bennis

PRINCIPLE: Your greatest impact comes not from the work you do—it comes from changing lives, including your own.

Enough about your team. Let's talk about you.

How much work do you do each day that you'll be proud of in ten years?

I'm not talking about whether your client or boss was pleased, or that you had a brilliant idea, or that you gained the acclaim of the people around you. I'm curious whether you'll be able to look back with pride on the sacrifices and choices that you made to bring that work into the world.

Oddly, many leaders cause a lot of harm in their pursuit of great work. They make compromises they would never have seen themselves making a few years prior. They step over people in order to

223

claim just a little more credit than they deserve. They neglect the lives of the people they care most about because they lose perspective. In truth, their pursuit of success eventually reveals what was really important to them all along.

When you envision success in your life, what do you see? Does it have something to do with your job title? How much money you make? Your lifestyle? The kind of work you do? Or does it have to do with the kind of impact you've made or the kind of person you are becoming?

Take a brief moment right now—just a handful of seconds—to pause and consider this question:

When I envision success, what do I see? (I'm serious—I'll wait right here.)

You see, many people don't have a clear definition of success in their own mind, so they spend their entire career—and much of their effort as a leader—chasing vapor. They navigate by gut, not by principle. They are drawn to opportunities that give them a sense of prestige or acclaim, whether that means more money, a better title, or more perks, and they lose sight of the body of work (and the life) they intended to build.

Some people measure success by their relative position to everyone around them. The next promotion is the only thing that matters, regardless of how they get there. Their definition of success looks something like: "I'm getting ahead of my peers."

Some people navigate their career by whatever will put the most zeroes at the end of their paycheck. Their definition of success is: "I have more money in the bank than most people I know."

Alternatively, some people just want stability. They take the most comfortable route, meaning work that they absolutely know they can do well, even if it means turning their back on opportunities that could allow them to magnify their impact. Their definition of success is "I have an easy, comfortable life."

Now, most people wouldn't readily admit to any of the above. If pressed, they will tell you how much they care about the work, about their team, and about how proud they are of the legacy they are leaving. I don't care what they say. I care what they do. The best way to determine what someone truly values is to examine the choices they make. Your choices tell the unvarnished truth about what really matters to you.

Many people don't have a clear definition of success in their own mind, so they spend their entire career . . . chasing vapor.

Up until now, this book has focused on your leadership of others and the principles by which healthy creative teams operate. However, a healthy team requires a leader with integrity. If you don't have a clear sense of who you are and where you are headed, then your team will eventually pay the price.

Integrity means very simply that your life is *integrated*. What is on the inside is plainly visible on the outside. There is no disparity between what you proclaim to value and what your actions prove. Your internal beliefs and external actions are aligned.

To lead with integrity, you have to resolve your own code of ethics—a private set of principles—that guide your decision making and help you navigate toward your true definition of success, rather than chasing opportunities that could potentially lure you off course. This set of principles may be similar to the ones that your team uses to guide its work, but it will also be different because it will be highly personal to you, your life situation, your ambitions, and most important, your deepest-held values. You *are* what you hold dearest.

What do you value most in the world and will never compromise?

How do you choose between two seemingly good options?

What battle lines have you drawn and refuse to cross?

Each of these questions is worth reflection, because each points to the deeper river that runs beneath the surface of your life. In moments of opportunity or when the pressure is on and you need someone to blame, it's easy to compromise these core values in order to protect yourself or grab at glory at the expense of your deeper principles. These small compromises are breaches of integrity that can eventually lead to a complete collapse. No one chooses to sell out what they care about. It happens in small ways over time.

Use your core values as a decision-making matrix to filter important choices. I was recently in New York City with a few hours to kill, and I decided to take a walk down Broadway to absorb the sights, sounds, and—yes—smells of the city. As I walked past a retail shop, a handful of people poured out onto the sidewalk in mid-conversation. As they passed behind me, I caught only a few sentences of their chatter before they mixed with the crowd and I lost them.

Man: "Wow! What did you do?"

Woman: "So, I lied to the pope. I had no choice."

[Record scratch]

OK, at this moment I had a thousand questions. For example:

Who *are* these people?

How did they get an audience with the pope?

Is my hearing going bad?

But more than anything, assuming I actually heard what I thought I heard, the thing I was most curious about was this: regardless of the circumstances, how do you get to a point where you feel like your only option is to lie to the pope?

I guarantee that if that ever happens to you, it won't be a "game time" decision. Big compromises are usually the result of smaller, seemingly insignificant compromises that eventually trap you. You become so immersed in a complex web of poor choices that it's difficult to see a reasonable path forward. Or because you haven't fully thought about what really matters, you eventually find yourself trapped in a corner, wondering how you got there.

If you don't understand what matters to you (your definition of success), then you are likely to be distracted by opportunities that will take you off course. Your decision-making matrix consists of the criteria that you use when making career decisions and, frankly, any decision in your life that could have an impact on your future. (I don't recommend filtering your lunch order through it.)

Again, your matrix might be tied to the principles by which your team operates, but at its core it represents your personal values, your beliefs, and your ambitions. For example, here are my three criteria when making a major career or life decision:

1. *Does it increase freedom for me and my stakeholders, or does it decrease it?* Our family places a very high priority on freedom. I want to be able to have the margin to say no when something doesn't feel right or when I believe it's not consistent with our definition of success. Money does not equate to freedom. Sometimes more income arrives with more strings attached, and it can actually inhibit our ability to live life in the way we wish. Because of this, I don't automatically take opportunities as they arise just because they will increase my profile or my bank account. I always take our family's freedom into account. (However, there are times when temporarily decreasing personal freedom is necessary in the pursuit of future

freedom—for example, taking on a project that requires a lot of travel in the short term but will give us margin later.)

Similarly, I seek opportunities in which I can engage in "freedom fighting" activities for others. I want my days to be about freeing up people to do their best work, whether that means helping them better align their team's systems, identify roadblocks, or surmount mental obstacles that stand in the way of greatness. This also determines how our family gives away its resources. We give a significant amount of our income (and time) each year to support organizations that engage in "freedom fighting," whether that means freeing slaves around the world, fighting poverty, or advocating for the powerless.

I tell you all of this not to say "hey—look what we're doing!" but because I want you to consider your *own* number one priority. If you are early in your career, freedom may not be a major consideration. You are still building your platform and trying to grow your skills and experience, and you are more concerned with how opportunities might open doors for you. Fantastic. But make sure that your criteria are known before you get into a situation in which you have to make a critical decision.

Big compromises are usually the result of smaller, seemingly insignificant compromises that eventually trap you.

2. *Is this a loving choice, or a selfish one?* I strive to serve. With every decision I make, I want to ensure that I am loving the people involved, not using them to achieve some end for me.

Love? How sappy and soft, right? Not really. Sometimes the loving decision is the one that temporarily hurts the other person, even though it's the right thing. Speaking truth to someone, especially when they don't want to hear it, can be an act of love. Even firing someone can be an act of love if you genuinely believe that it's in the person's best interest. (In these instances, the manner in which you do the act is key as well.)

There are times when a corporation seeks to hire me in an area where I don't have the appropriate expertise, or I know that I can't commit the appropriate time to do right by them. Truthfully, I could probably take the work and do just fine, but I know that I'm not really the best choice and that someone else could do a far better job, and maybe less expensively. In these instances, I turn down the work as an act of "love" rather than selfishly agreeing to do it just for the sake of financial gain or prestige. To me, this is a matter of integrity.

With regard to big decisions, I always ask: "Is there a loving choice?" Sometimes the answer is "not really," but there are times I realize that it's a choice between using someone else to gain an advantage or loving them.

3. Does it multiply my impact? The third criterion, which is often the only one that people consider, is whether it will increase my platform for impact, open new opportunities to pursue my productive passion, or help me achieve my business goals. Listen, unless your parents left you a trust fund, you have to work for a living. (Even in that case, you'll probably still be driven to work, because humans are wired to create value.) Increasing your influence and profile in your organization or industry is a very good thing, provided that it's not your only criterion. I intentionally seek opportunities that will improve my visibility, gain acclaim for my work, and increase my ability to have more impact through what I do.

So if I can answer in the affirmative to all three of these—it results in more freedom, it's the loving (or neutral) choice, and it multiplies my impact—then it's a no-brainer yes for me. However, if any of these three results in a no, the choice isn't so easy. If it results in less freedom, we have to consider whether the benefit of the other two criteria justifies the decision. If it is a choice available to me only because the person offering it is naive or incompetent, then it's an automatic no. If it doesn't multiply my impact, but it results in more freedom or is a loving choice, it still might be a yes, but only after consideration.

Whatever your decision-making criteria are, please have some. Then, once you've resolved them, privately filter your important decisions through them. Never violate your personal ethics in order to achieve temporal gain. It's not worth it.

Take time each quarter to assess your life, your leadership, and how consistently you're living out your values. Life and work come at you fast, so it is invaluable to have some regular rhythms to help you assess how you're progressing toward your definition of success.

Spend some focused time thinking about your values, your career, and where you are headed. What kinds of experiences do you want to have? What kind of work would you eventually like to be doing? With whom would you like to work?

Come to terms with acceptable compromises now, before you're under pressure. Many big career blunders are made because people simply don't know what they want or, worse, what they're willing to accept. It's important to know yourself and understand what you're willing to accept if your ideal career path isn't placed in front of you. Make sure that you have a firm understanding of what you're willing to accept before you agree to take a role that—although it might pay better or offer more prestige—tempts you to compromise your core values.

I recommend that you take a full day once a quarter as a checkpoint and consider some of the ideas above. I know that sounds like a lot, especially if you're in a busy season, but a little bit of analysis and course correction now is better than a ton of corrective action later. During your checkpoint, get alone (whether in your office or off-site) and engage in the questions and rituals that have been presented throughout the book. (A cheat sheet is in the back.) Additionally, I challenge you to ask the following:

What big decisions are on the horizon? Filter them through your personal decision-making criteria and anticipate how you might respond.

Is my leadership consistent with my values? If not, how can I better align?

As you become more steeped in what you really value—your *true* definition of success—your decision making will become much more consistent, and your team's trust will grow.

Find your council of advisers. Finally, do you have a group of people around you who help you think through your important decisions and critical crossroads? When you are flying solo, your perspective is limited, and there is a good chance that you'll miss important considerations, even ones that are obvious to everyone

> **Never violate your personal ethics in order to achieve temporal gain. It's not worth it.**

around you. Identify a small group of trusted advisers who understand what you value, have some context for the work you are doing, and who care about you enough that they are willing to speak the truth to you even when you won't like it.

Dave Munson's company makes great leather bags. I've traveled all over the world with one of his Saddleback Leather briefcases, and it's by far my favorite bag I've ever owned. Munson didn't set out to be a leatherpreneur. In fact, his company started by accident. He was teaching English in a Mexican village, and he wanted a bag—"one like Indiana Jones might carry"—for transporting books and papers to and from the school. Munson couldn't find one that looked like what he wanted, so he sketched a bag himself and hired a leather shop owner to create it. When he would travel back to the United States, others would comment about how much they loved his bag and asked where they could buy one. He immediately commissioned the leather worker to create a handful more bags for him, and he sold them online and during his trips home. Soon he realized that there was a great opportunity and started Saddleback Leather to sell goods that—in his words—"people will fight over when you're dead."

Things were not so smooth for the company at the beginning. Munson was having difficulty delegating responsibility to new team members, and he wasn't quite sure how to scale a business that was based on selling high-quality products, so he hired someone to coach him. His coach helped him see things that weren't immediately apparent to him, such as uneven work distribution within his business, and pointed out ways in which he was actually working against his business instead of for it.

"Seek wisdom," Munson told me. "Ask for help. People want to help. Raise your hand and say, 'Excuse me, I don't know how to do this. Can you help me?'" He said that the decision to ask someone to reveal the reality of what was going on in the business was the greatest decision he made early in the life of his business. It saved him from burning himself out and running the company into the ground.

Who reveals reality to you? Is there someone in your life with more experience than you who has permission to see everything that's going on and to offer his perspective on how you might do things better? This is different from a typical "mentorship" role. A mentor only has so much visibility into your life and work and usually only has a limited role in offering advice. Mentors tend to remain at a distance rather than getting their hands dirty with you and helping you figure things out. They often don't really have "skin in the game." You need someone who is really invested in your success and is willing to tell you things you don't want to hear, then stick around to make sure that you actually act on that advice.

I recommend that your council of advisers not be from your organization, because you want to know that their advice is coming from a place of genuine concern for *you*, not just the company. Also, these aren't just your friends, who will likely tell you what you want to hear. Strive to find advisers with a diverse set of experiences or who come from different industries. Buy them a drink (or two) and ask them to offer their perspective on your dilemma. Tell them you will do the same for them, when the time comes.

If you implement these three suggestions (identify your decision-making matrix, engage in regular checkpoints, and maintain a council of advisers), you are much less likely to be drawn off course by a shiny opportunity. Thus, you are much more likely to build a body of work that's consistent with your values and that you'll point to with pride in ten years. More important, you'll be a leader with integrity who is consistent regardless of the corporate political climate, team dynamics, or your position.

YOUR ROLE IS NOT WHO YOU ARE

Jane Chen is the cofounder of Embrace Innovations, a company that's created an innovative product called the Embrace Warmer. It helps mothers of premature babies living in developing countries keep their baby warm at the fraction of the cost of a typical incubator, and it's a complete game changer. In the early days of the company, she moved to India with her team in order to launch the company and to be closer to those who needed her lifesaving product. All seemed to be going very well, and it looked like plans to find someone to take the company to the next level of impact were being solidified. Chen was ready to take a breath. She moved back to the United States from India to go on a sabbatical, contingent upon finishing a deal with a major multinational health-care company. This deal was going to secure the company for the immediate future and was the culmination of six years of work. However, things didn't quite go as planned. Just one week before signing the deal, the company fired their health-care CEO and pulled the plug on the financing.

Chen said that this disastrous turn of events almost sank Embrace. "We had seven days of cash left, and we'd taken out bridge loans to make ends meet." Everyone was telling her that it was time to close the company, but she refused to accept their advice. She called every single person she knew, asking for small investments just to get the company through another day. Embrace had gone from imminent and sustainable success to nearly inevitable failure in just a matter of days.

Then she remembered that she had met Mark Benioff of Salesforce.com nine months earlier. Coincidentally, Benioff was interested in this issue and was about to make a contribution to the Gates Foundation to create a global program to help premature babies.

Chen e-mailed Benioff during the crisis to share what was going on with Embrace, and she entered into discussions with his team. At this critical juncture, he agreed to help fund them. "His belief in the company and trust in me was unbelievable, and if it weren't for him this company wouldn't exist today."

Although the outcome for Embrace and all of those who depend on its technology was remarkable, Chen said that the personal learning she took from the crisis has shaped her outlook on work and leadership in profound ways. "I realized that I had become so attached to the end outcome that I let it define my whole identity. Now, I still give my work everything I've got, but I realize I don't always have the agency to control the outcomes."

You can do everything right, have a clear and compelling vision, build a brilliant team, and keep them inspired and productive, and—in the end—you can still fail to hit your objectives. There are simply too many factors beyond your control. However, what you can't do is allow your identity to become subsumed into your job title or your role. If that happens, you will do anything necessary in order to protect your turf, regardless of how that affects everyone around you. Also, your motivation and sense of purpose will rise and fall with your victories and successes, and there will be no consistent foundation for your work other than how it makes you feel in the moment. You must maintain a healthy level of detachment from the work while simultaneously stoking the fires of your passion for greatness.

Question: Are you overidentifying with your role? Do you feel the need to protect your turf?

HOLD YOUR ROLE LOOSELY

My family and I live in Cincinnati. It's a beautiful, small(ish) city perched on the banks of the Ohio River and nestled in the foothills of southern Ohio. One of the little-known tidbits of trivia about Cincinnati is how it got its name. (Some people assume it's a Native American name, but it's not.) Cincinnati is named for Lucius Quinctius Cincinnatus, the legendary Roman leader. Cincinnatus, who was retired, was approached by the Roman senate at a time of great turmoil. The Roman army had been battling its neighbors and was surrounded. They pleaded with Cincinnatus to accept the role of dictator and to lead the remainder of the army against the enemy. As the story goes, when the contingent sent to inform him of the decision finally found him, he was plowing his fields.

Cincinnatus accepted his charge and proceeded to win a decisive victory. That alone would be a remarkable story: "Farmer Becomes Dictator and Wins Battle." That would play well in Hollywood.

However, the true reason Cincinnatus is a legend and has cities named in his honor is what happened next. Immediately upon his return from battle, Cincinnatus relinquished his role as dictator and resumed his life on the farm. At the height of his power, when he could have demanded anything he wanted, he surrendered it all and resumed his humble life.

In the days following the Revolutionary War, George Washington and others formed the Society of the Cincinnati, in honor of Cincinnatus. Washington was the society's president. It's no wonder that he, at the height of his power, also stepped down as president of the United States when he could have dictated anything he desired.

The story of Cincinnatus has always inspired me, but lately it's taken on new meaning as I've been considering the urgent importance of self-forgetfulness in leadership. The role of a leader is to be so obsessively focused on the mission that others can't help but follow along. The leader gets to make the most sacrifices. The moment that those who follow sense that there is a personal agenda at the heart of the leader's actions, trust and respect are broken. There has to be something more at stake than "What can I get from this?" Great leaders bend their life around a vision that's more important than pay or prestige and conduct themselves with integrity regardless of the pressure to compromise. They strive for impact, not monuments.

DON'T BUILD MONUMENTS. MAKE ECHOES.

If you have a heartbeat, you probably aspire to continually advance in your career. Very few talented people are content to stay in one role for years. However, the best way to grow your influence is to prove yourself competent with the work you've already been given. If you constantly have one eye on your work and one eye on the work you *wish* you were doing, you'll eventually begin to drop balls. Your true ambition will eventually show through. However, if you commit yourself to fully and completely doing the work you've been assigned, seek to develop new skills whenever you can in the course of your work, and show yourself to be loyal to the organization and its mission, even when it's at personal cost, then you position yourself well for the next phase of your career.

Great leaders bend their life around a vision that's more important than pay or prestige and conduct themselves with integrity regardless of the circumstances.

I don't mean to sound naive. This is far from the killer shark kinds of career advice that you often hear from gurus and titans of industry. However, I'm assuming three things about you: (1) you actually care about the work and the people you are leading, (2) you aspire to have a life beyond your job and want to set an example for your loved ones, and (3) your character matters more to you than a little bit of temporary success.

This is not a game you're playing. How you choose to engage your work as a leader has massive ramifications. Conduct yourself in a manner that you'll be proud of in ten years, not in whatever way lets you score arbitrary points here and now. The greatest impact you make on the world will not be the things you made or the products you brought to market. It won't even be the company you helped build. The greatest impact you make will be the lives that are changed through your leadership, which happens as you build into and empower the people who follow you.

I'm reminded of Percy Shelley's sonnet "Ozymandias," which describes the ruins of a statue of a once great ruler, now sitting isolated in desert sands and forgotten by history.

> And on the pedestal these words appear:
> "My name is Ozymandias, king of kings:
> Look on my works, ye Mighty, and despair!"
> Nothing beside remains. Round the decay
> Of that colossal wreck, boundless and bare
> The lone and level sands stretch far away.

How easy it is to build monuments to ourselves and to fight to make ourselves known through the work that we do. There's nothing wrong with wanting to do great work, but it's important to recognize that all but a handful of the best-known companies and leaders of today will be completely forgotten in a hundred years. If you spend your life trying to build a name for yourself at all cost, there will indeed be a tremendous cost to be paid. However, those leaders who commit themselves to developing the people around them—unleashing *their* potential, helping them recognize *their* own greatness, and teaching them to curb their destructive impulses—will build a body of work that echoes down through generations as their influence multiplies through the lives of the people they've led.

Be a leader who makes echoes.

ACKNOWLEDGMENTS

It takes a few years to type a book, but many more years to actually formulate the ideas inside of one. Thanks to the many people who lent their ideas and years of experience to this project. Specifically, thanks to Brian Koppelman, Kirk Perry, Lisa Johnson, Bill Taylor, Jane Chen, Dave Munson, David Wiser, Sean Heritage, Nathan Hendricks, Chris Andruss, Kelly Smith, Ben Nicholson, Jeremy Bailey, Josh Banko, Rick Hensley, Jim Friedman, Rob Rivenburgh, Michael Bungay Stanier, Scott Mautz, riCardo Crespo, Cal Newport, Adam Steltzner, and Chris Michel for sharing your insights in one way or another. Also, thanks to the dozens of people whose insights and stories are shared (often with changed names) throughout these pages.

A book goes through many lives and passes through many hands before it's released. Thanks to my (brilliant) editors Niki Papadopoulos and Vivian Roberson for helping me find my voice, and for your vision for the project and your very direct feedback along the way. Also, thanks to Adrian Zackheim and Will Weisser for your continued vote of confidence, and Margot Stamas and Alyson Hancock for helping me get this book into the world.

ACKNOWLEDGMENTS

Thanks to my wonderful and hardworking literary agent, Melissa Sarver-White. Also, thanks to Tom Neilssen, Les Tuerk, Michele DiLisio, Adam Kirschenbaum, and the entire team at Brightsight Group for keeping me in front of audiences with whom I can share my ideas.

I'm grateful to my family for their continued patience and support during the writing and editing processes. I love you.

Finally, thanks to all of the leaders out there braving the storm and striving to bring brilliant work into the world each day. You are changing the very world around you.

LIST OF RITUALS

Throughout the book, you encountered numerous checkpoints to help you implement the ideas in each chapter. Below is a comprehensive list of the weekly, monthly, and quarterly rituals mentioned in each chapter. Don't try to do all of them at each checkpoint. Rather, select a few that you think might benefit you most and concentrate on those.

WEEKLY

—Do a mental sweep of the past week for times when you shifted into maker mode versus manager mode and consider how it affected the team dynamic.

—Do a quick scan of your principles or leadership philosophy and consider any areas where you or the team might be violating them.

—As you look at your upcoming schedule, consider any meetings or situations where you might encounter a power imbalance. How will you make everyone involved feel engaged and permitted to bring their best ideas? (This could mean having conversations ahead of time to encourage them to speak or being extra careful to put your gun away during the meeting.)

—Schedule a one-on-one coaching meeting with at least one person on your team this week. Listen to them and help them identify areas for growth.

—Reflect on current projects and where you may be allowing expectation escalation to overwhelm the rhythm of your team. Are you setting bait-and-switch expectations with your team?

—Consider your current project work, and whether your team has a clear understanding of roles, expectations, and strategy.

—Choose one cultural principle that you will elevate this week. Find ways of working it into your conversation.

—Consider each member of your team and the problems he or she is tasked with solving. Are the problems clearly defined?

—Look at your upcoming calendar and shift the schedule so that your team has blocks of time for focused work.

—Send an e-mail with a key resource or article to your team, and explain why you're sending it. Make sure it's something that will inspire them to think in new ways about the work, or open their minds to new possibilities.

—Set up your weekly schedule around when you will do your own deep work, which could involve strategy, team planning, or getting ahead of the team's work. Encourage your team to do the same.

—Take some time to consider the interactions on your team and note where there are any potential conflicts or signs of dissension.

MONTHLY

—Review your scoreboard and dashboard and revise them as needed.

—Spend some time considering the marks of good leadership. (For example, from chapter 1: *a good leader of creative people accomplishes the objectives while developing the team's ability to shoulder new and more challenging work.*) Do you feel like you are accomplishing these right now, or is there an area you need to work on?

—Invite someone on your team to connect with you over lunch or coffee with the sole purpose of getting to know them better and understand their aspirations.

—Consider someplace where your team has fallen short of its objectives. Schedule a time to discuss the failure and what you learned from it. Don't make this intimidating; make it as light and casual as possible.

—Consider the past month of work. Have there been any breaches of trust on your part? Do you need to make it right with someone?

—As you look at your upcoming workload, consider the key decisions that will need to be made and when they will need to be made so that you can stay ahead of your team's work.

—Consider your team culture and where you need to prune. Are there any deviations from expected behavior that are in danger of becoming normalized?

—Consider the upcoming projects your team will be working on and establish clear challenges (problem statements) for each.

—Eliminate something from the calendar or tasks list this month so that your team has more time and attention for its most valuable projects.

—Consider what resources you can add to your team's "stimulus library" to help them stay inspired. What have you read or watched recently that you wish more of your team had access to?

—Take a look at all of your recurring meetings and time commitments. What has outlived its effectiveness and needs to be pruned?

—Have a conversation with your core team members about their level of satisfaction with the work and the team's overall dynamics.

QUARTERLY

—Choose one to two projects that you will give yourself permission to stay directly involved in so that you don't become too disconnected from the work.

—Review your guiding principles to make sure that they are still relevant and comprehensive.

—Do a broad review of your relationships on your team and note any relational awkwardness or power imbalances that have developed.

—Consider the rhythm of your coaching conversations and your team's response to them. Have you seen growth in your team over the past few months? If not, how do you need to challenge individual team members to step out of their comfort zone?

—Identify a few stories from your past that you might want to share with the team at an opportune time. These can be times you failed and learned something, a story from your childhood, or anything else that humanizes you to the team.

—Consider your team's project work from a higher perspective. Are you hitting your marks? Is your team healthy? Are team members developing and growing in their capacity to do more and better work?

—As you look at your team's upcoming rhythm, consider the cultural principles that you want to elevate and reward over the coming quarter. How will you do so?

—Take time to think about areas of potential misalignment or assumptive behavior on your team. Are you sensing a growing gap between the *what* and the *why* of your work?

—Review your team's meeting schedule and organizational commitments—prune aggressively.

—Plan a stimulus dive for your team around a big project.

—Reconsider your team's meetings and who's invited to each. Do you need to make any changes?

—Reiterate your team's core principles, and review the rules of fair fighting.

—You: *What big decisions are on the horizon?* Filter them through your personal decision-making criteria and anticipate how you might respond.

—You: *Is my leadership consistent with my values? If not, how can I better align?*

NEXT STEPS AND RESOURCES

Visit ToddHenry.com/herdingtigers for:

Notes and Suggested Reading
We've compiled reference notes by chapter, recommended reading, and additional resources to help you further explore the topic of creative leadership.

The Leader List
This is a short weekly e-mail designed to help you apply the principles in this book.

The Workbook
We've created a set of worksheets to help you apply the principles in *Herding Tigers* with question prompts, suggested conversations to have with your team, and more. The workbook is designed to help you focus on one principle per week.

Group Resources and Materials
If you'd like to study *Herding Tigers* with your team, we have question prompts and suggested best practices for your group discussion.

Visit ToddHenry.com for:

Keynotes and Workshops
Let us help you unleash your team's best work, unlock its creative potential, spark your passion, and collaborate more effectively.

Podcasts
Join tens of thousands who subscribe to *The Accidental Creative* podcast for a weekly dose of advice about how to stay prolific, brilliant, and healthy.

INDEX

Also available from Todd Henry

For details visit www.ToddHenry.com/books.